Working Together in Law

Working Together in Law

Teamwork and Small Group Skills for Legal Professionals

Eileen Scallen
Sophie Sparrow
Cliff Zimmerman

CAROLINA ACADEMIC PRESS
Durham, North Carolina

Library of Congress Cataloging-in-Publication Data

Scallen, Eileen A.
  Working together in Law : teamwork and small group skills for legal profes-
sionals / Eileen Scallen, Sophie Sparrow, and Cliff Zimmerman.
    pages cm
  Includes bibliographical references and index.
  ISBN 978-1-59460-591-8 (alk. paper)
  1. Practice of law--United States. 2. Teams in the workplace--United States.
I. Sparrow, Sophie. II. Zimmerman, Cliff. III. Title.

KF300.S29 2013
340.068'4--dc23   2013018721

CAROLINA ACADEMIC PRESS
700 Kent Street
Durham, North Carolina 27701
Telephone (919) 489-7486
Fax (919) 493-5668
www.cap-press.com

Printed in the United States of America

Contents

Preface

I am a lawyer and law professor. I love thinking and writing about legal communication, both argumentation and persuasion, the arts of influence. I started this book project because I never felt that way about small group work, or, perish the thought, "teamwork." Without dating myself completely, I am a pre-Title IX woman, so I did not have the same opportunities as my three brothers to play on sports teams. Thus, "teamwork" was not part of my vocabulary for most of my personal and professional life. I was cynical about terms such as "teamwork" and "leadership" because they are easier to put on posters than to put into practice. I do not feel the same way after working on this book. Let me try to explain why I have changed.

I wanted to be a lawyer from the time I was six years old. Before I went to law school, however, I obtained a master's degree in Communication Studies and taught basic public speaking at the University of Minnesota. During my graduate school program, I carefully avoided all organizational and small group communication courses. I knew the arts of argumentation and persuasion were fundamental to law, and that was where I was headed. I did not want to waste my time on the "soft" skills of collaborative work. However, in law school, in legal practice, and in law teaching, I kept finding myself working in groups and teams: editing the law review, working on joint defense teams in practice, or serving on academic committees. No matter how much I wished I could, I could not learn, practice, or teach law all by myself.

About the time I was realizing the importance of collaborative work to my life in the law, one of my close friends, Tony Robb-John, left his entertainment law practice to obtain his M.B.A. at the London Business School. Most of his work in business school was done in teams. He shared his passion for teamwork with me, and lamented that he had received no training in working well in groups or teams in law school. I realized that he was right. The vast majority of law schools, both in the U.S. and the UK, do not emphasize small group communication skills. Law schools have always taught argumentation and persuasion, but teaching students to "think like a lawyer" also means teaching them to communicate like a lawyer, in writing and in public forums. For quite some time, law schools have been teaching public speaking in trial advocacy and moot courts. More recently, we have started teaching other communication skills, such as negotiation and interviewing. Many of us now assign students to work on group projects in class or clinics, but we rarely stop to teach those students how to work effectively with others, particularly when they do not get to control every aspect of a project. And we rarely have our students reflect on why some of their group work experiences are more successful than others.

My experience as a law professor has been shaped by the two law schools where I have served as both a faculty member and as an administrator. I began my career as a faculty member and administrator at the University of California, Hastings College of the Law. At Hastings, I found a culture of strong faculty governance and an intellectual community. I did not fully realize it then, but I started absorbing intellectual and practical lessons about working collaboratively at Hastings, even though I taught mostly large doctrinal courses in Civil Procedure and Evidence. I left Hastings in 2000 for family reasons and returned to my home state of Minnesota to join the faculty of William Mitchell College of Law in Saint Paul, Minnesota. Almost everything I know about skills training, I learned from my colleagues at William Mitchell. Here is a small part of what they have taught me: when it comes to learning communication skills, whether writing, public speaking, negotiating, or working in groups and teams, a few individuals seem to be naturally gifted. They excel at the skill almost unconsciously. While the vast majority of law students, lawyers, judges, and law professors may not be "gifted," they generally do have some innate ability with language, which is why they chose to enter the legal profession, and so they have the capacity to improve. We can study, practice, reflect, practice harder, and improve substantially at particular communication skills. And just because someone has talent in one type of communication does not mean that individual will be equally gifted in all communication situations. I have been told I am an excellent public speaker. I am a reasonably good negotiator. But I was not as comfortable with small group and team work; I knew I could be a more effective communicator in those settings.

So, I saw a need, in the legal profession and in myself. There is a maxim in education: "The best way to learn something is to teach it to someone else."

Thus, in the summer of 2003, Tony Robb-John and I taught an experiential class on "Team Leadership for Lawyers," with the enthusiastic support of my then-Dean, Harry Haynsworth and Vice Dean, Matthew P. Downs, at William Mitchell College of Law. William Mitchell students are used to the hard work of practical skills courses, but they were challenged by the experience of depending on each other to produce complex legal work. When Tony and I saw their frustration as we guided them through the course, we muttered to each other, "Welcome to the practice of law." Tony and I began to plot out this book to help law students and lawyers feel more comfortable and be more effective working in small groups and teams.

Tony and I realized that we could not write this book by ourselves. When I started to research the literature about teaching law students to work in groups, I found Cliff Zimmerman's work about teaching law students to write collaboratively, and read about his work on incorporating team skills in the curriculum at Northwestern University School of Law. Cliff was exceedingly busy, professionally and personally, when I first approached him about helping on this book. But he was gracious enough to start coaching me through what turned out to be a long, grueling writing process, and he ended up getting far more involved in the book than I think he had planned! When Tony Robb-John could not make sufficient time from his international transactional practice to continue working on the book, we knew the team needed another member.

I found Sophie Sparrow, Professor of Law at the University of New Hampshire, through her teaching and contributions to the Team-Based Learning Collaborative. (http://www.teambasedlearning.org). This nonprofit organization pulls together educators from business, medicine, engineering, the humanities, and increasingly from law, to learn from each other how best to engage our students in actively applying the concepts and theories of our diverse disciplines, and in the process, how to work well collaboratively with their future professional colleagues. Even though she too had a full schedule, teaching, writing, and being a law teaching consultant, Sophie gladly made time to work on this book with us.

When I reflect on the ensuing writing process, I have to laugh. When we practiced what we preach in this book, things went reasonably well. I pulled together and sifted through an enormous amount of research from business, psychology, sociology, and communication studies. Sophie kept us organized and on schedule, or schedules, as we repeatedly modified them. Cliff brought his rich experience with guiding years of teaching law students to write well together, and kept my spirits up when I questioned why we were doing this book. Tony continued to provide stories and encouragement from across the Atlantic.

However, when we lost sight of the principles we put forth in the book, we experienced confusion over content, miscommunication, relationship repair work, and delays. We struggled with the demands of finishing this book along with all our other professional obligations, and the ups and downs of everyday life, such as children moving through adolescence into college, family and personal illness, career issues, and house renovation. I have never undertaken such a frustrating, lengthy, and grueling writing project. And I have never learned so much from one or felt such satisfaction upon completion.

In working on this book, I learned that I do not have to be a sparkling team player to be an effective group member. I discovered that when you become an effective group member you are more likely to help the group become a successful team. I also learned that you do not have to be in charge to be a leader in a group of others. Everyone in the group should help lead it to success, and that leadership can and will shift and change over the course of the project. In the end, I understand that group and teamwork are part of the everyday work life of every legal professional working in the 21st century. I cannot avoid group and team work. Not by being a lawyer. Not even by being a law professor. Most important, I learned that I do not want to avoid small groups or teams any longer.

Now I understand why I should have embraced working in groups and teams long ago. I still believe that it is far easier to talk about the value of teamwork (or put it on a poster or coffee mug) than to do it. However, I know now that when collaborative work is done thoughtfully, the group likely will create better work than an individual working alone. Moreover, there is great pleasure in working with thoughtful, funny, and talented individuals when you have systems and skills for managing conflict and work on building relationships. My personal and professional life has been enriched by working on the team that produced this book. As a result, I no longer dread collaborative work. In fact, given the right situation (see the material that follows, not all work is suited for collaboration), I seek it out. One more thing: I now play ice hockey on women's teams. It is never too late to learn new skills.

Eileen A. Scallen,
St. Paul, Minnesota. February, 2013

Acknowledgments

My Myers-Briggs type is INFP. You can learn more about what that means when you read Chapter 2. But one thing it means is that I first prefer to think about and communicate "the big picture." My personal life and my career as a lawyer and law professor have been shaped by the many large and small organizations through which I have learned to work collaboratively—whether I wanted to or not. I cannot begin to name them all here, but here are some of the most influential: the graduate and professional schools to which I have belonged as a student, administrator, and faculty member, the University of Minnesota, Twin Cities (Communication Studies and Law), the University of California, Hastings College of the Law, and William Mitchell College of Law; my former legal employers, the Chambers of the Honorable A. Wallace Tashima, then-U.S. District Judge for the Central District of California, and the law firm of Latham & Watkins; my pro bono and public service clients, Twin Cities Pride, OutFront Minnesota, and the National Center for Lesbian Rights; and, most recently, my women's ice hockey teams, to date, Babes on Blades, the Bombers, and Penalty Box ("Go Boxers!").

Zooming in from the big picture, there are individuals who I proudly count as honorary teammates on this book project. Anthony Robb-John hatched and developed the idea for this book with me, as I discuss in the Preface, and supported me throughout the process of writing it. My former colleagues at William Mitchell College of Law, Dean Harry Haynsworth and Vice Dean Matthew P. Downs, supported this project enthusiastically from the beginning—demonstrating strong collaborative skills themselves! The administrators and editors at Carolina Academic Press embraced this book when other publishers rejected it, saying, "But no one has written about that, how would we market it?" Cal Bonde and Linda Thorstad at the Faculty Publications Department at William Mitchell College of Law prepared the manuscript for publication with grace and the utmost professionalism. Cody Zustiak, William Mitchell College of Law '13, provided research assistance and copy editing with efficiency and cheerfulness. The staff of the library at William Mitchell College of Law sought out information and interlibrary loans, helping with social science and management theory research far beyond the typical law school resources. My friends and family, the most important groups in my life, especially Marianne Norris, my life partner, provided the love that sustains me through good times and bad. Finally, my co-authors on this book, Sophie Sparrow and Cliff Zimmerman, have taught me more than they will ever realize about the importance and joy of legal professionals working well together. Thank you, all of you.

Eileen A. Scallen, St. Paul, Minnesota, February 2013

My deep thanks go to the many attorneys who graciously and generously spoke to me about their collaborative experiences in practice; you inspire me to continue teaching students about effective collaboration. I also deeply appreciate the support of the University of New Hampshire and the assistance of Matthew Burrows, JD '13, in preparing this book. And I am extremely grateful to my family, Chris, Kai and Silas, for all their support and patience while I was working on this book. Above all, I thank my many students who have engaged in multiple kinds of groupwork and teamwork and taught me more than I could ever have learned on my own.

Sophie Sparrow, Concord, New Hampshire, February 2013

Every group writing effort has been both challenging and rewarding for me. And I would not trade those experiences because the rewards are great and enduring. Life is about working in teams. The most gratifying experiences are personal. Thanks to Dea, Ben, and Nina for your ever-present love and support through all my ventures. High on the list are the academic experiences as well. I greatly appreciate the support of Northwestern University School of Law. Even more, I am indebted to the students whom I have taught and who have taught me over the years. In particular I want to thank Adam Hopson JD/MBA '13, for his excellent research and editing. His perspective on the draft read was invaluable. I want to also thank Cameron Mazzetta, Kent State University '14, and Nina Zimmerman, Kenyon College '14, for their research during the summer of 2011. Their efforts combined with their desire to learn and pressing me to help them understand collaboration provided yet another enlightening group work experience.

Cliff Zimmerman, Chicago, Illinois, February 2013

Working Together in Law

Chapter 1

Lawyers as Leaders in the 21st Century

1.1 · The Myth of the Legal "Lone Ranger"

Conjure up images of famous fictional and nonfictional lawyers, especially the favorable ones. Classic fictional lawyers—like Atticus Finch in *To Kill a Mockingbird*, TV's Perry Mason, Harriet ("Harry's Law") Korn, or Susan Sarandon's character in the film *The Client*—all stand alone. Or picture real lawyers, past and present:

- Clarence Darrow, who represented the teacher of evolution in the Scopes Monkey Trial immortalized in the play *Inherit the Wind*;
- Gloria Allred, who has sued many celebrities and politicians;
- Bella Abzug, Congresswoman who advocated for women's rights;
- Johnnie Cochran, who represented O.J. Simpson and other high profile criminal defendants;
- Gerry Spence, noted criminal defense attorney who claims he never lost a case;
- Barbara Jordan, noted Congresswoman and orator;
- David Boies, who has had many high profile cases and clients, including presidential candidate Al Gore, who lost the Supreme Court case of *Bush v. Gore*; or
- Ted Olson, former Solicitor General, the winning counsel in *Bush v. Gore*, and most recently, joint counsel with his former opponent, David Boies, in the Supreme Court case challenging California's ban on same-sex marriage. (*Hollingsworth v. Perry*, 2012).

We usually think of them only as individuals. But how realistic are these images of the solitary legal mind? Successful lawyers today rarely work alone.

Legal work in the 21st century is more complex and more time-pressured than ever before. Lawyers are expected to engage in 24/7 communication, thanks to the lowering of trade barriers, globalization, and in-house counsels' increasing demands for efficiency. All of these factors mean that lawyers' work is changing. A few examples illustrate this:

- **Disaster response litigation.** The regulatory and civil litigation proceedings resulting from the attack on the World Trade Center Towers, the aftermath of Hurricane Katrina and Superstorm Sandy, and the BP oil spill. All involved enormous teams of lawyers in law firms, government agencies, and regulatory bodies all around the world.
- **Nongovernmental organizations ("NGOs") and nonprofit legal organizations.** Professor Dale Carpenter described the teamwork among sixteen different organizations that filed *amicus* briefs in the case of *Lawrence v. Texas*, urging the U.S. Supreme Court to strike down the Texas law criminalizing sodomy between same-sex couples. (Carpenter, 2012). The lead organization representing the gay defendants in the case, Lambda Legal, had to designate one of its lawyers to coordinate the amicus briefs from groups ranging from historians, to libertarians and supportive Republican organizations, to gay-friendly religious groups, to leading psychological and medical professional organizations. Teamwork was crucial here, as is often the case in high-profile litigation, because the arguments in these briefs needed not only to reflect the main theories of the case, but also make independent contributions expressing the distinct voices of the organizations submitting them.
- **Mergers and acquisitions.** Lawyers in private practice work not only in their own law-firm teams but also on teams with other firms, and of course, with the in-house counsel and client teams—commonly, around the clock and around the world.
- **White collar crime prosecution.** In the case against international business leader Rajat Gupta, former head of McKinsey and director at Goldman Sachs. Prosecution and defense teams were composed of several disciplines, including forensic investigators, accounting and finance experts, and lawyers from multiple firms or government agencies, all working as part of legal teams.

The conclusion we draw is that the sun has set on the day of the Lone Ranger lawyer—assuming that this character ever truly existed. Even Perry Mason had his loyal secretary Della Street and investigator Paul Drake. Johnnie Cochran was one part of O.J. Simpson's "Dream Team," along with Robert Shapiro, F. Lee Bailey, Gerald Uelmen, Barry Scheck, Peter Neufeld, and many others.

We interviewed a number of lawyers and legal professionals from a wide range of practice areas for this book, asking them to discuss their experiences working in small groups and teams. You will find their stories throughout this book. But their overarching message was that it is essential for law students and lawyers to develop the skills necessary for working well with others. The former General Counsel of an entrepreneurial company with global markets put it this way:

> Young attorneys think that understanding the law is sufficient. It is necessary, but not sufficient. We don't talk about the other skills.... A lot of work gets done in teams. Regular working groups, such as the legal group, the senior management team, and assigned cross-functional task-oriented teams. Cross-functional teams have a problem to solve, such as how to deal with changing environment regulations, and how to make sure that the claims about the product are true. Within the company, a lawyer is often on one of the teams.... Being successful in-house depends on the skills of influence. Just because you're a lawyer and you say it, doesn't mean that people will do it. Trust is key.

Practicing lawyers are not the only team players in the legal profession. Individuals with law degrees are found in corporate and nonprofit organizations where teamwork is more openly acknowledged and rewarded. We talk about "panels" of appellate court judges, without thinking of them as members of teams, but they certainly are—even though they might cringe at being called a team. Even administrative law judges or trial court judges, whether state or federal, work with colleagues on a wide range of committees aimed at improving the quality of justice in an era of diminishing resources. To be successful in this century, lawyers need to develop leadership skills that allow them to work effectively with others.

When we talk about "lawyers" in this book we include all types of legal professionals. Anyone who works with people who have a law degree, including law professors and law school deans is a "lawyer." We are specifically concerned with those who have a law degree because they have the opportunity during law school to develop the fundamental leadership skills they need to work effectively with others. As we discuss more below, we know that law schools, including our own, have been remiss in providing this training until recently. We want to provide a resource that will help current law students and those who are using their law degrees today in a variety of settings in which they must work collaboratively with others.

Today's legal professionals still have plenty of solitary work: individual research and analysis, drafting, writing, and speaking. But today's lawyer is often part of a working team. In this chapter, we use the terms "working collaboratively," "working with others," "working in groups," and "working in teams" interchangeably. In Chapter Three, we illustrate the difference between working in groups and being part of an effective team.

Today's lawyers work in groups that use electronic or virtual communication as part of its normal means of interacting with one another. One government lawyer we spoke with is an example of this reality. This lawyer works for a public agency with about 500 employees. She estimated she spent 75–95% of her job working with other people. She works with a large variety of people, mostly non-lawyers, on many projects. Most of her day is spent working on cross-functional teams, monitoring consent decrees, collecting data, drafting policy, solving problems, and working on compliance issues. We have seen this in our own work. From the largest law firms to the smallest, from media companies to law schools, and in the United States, England, and throughout the world, legal professionals increasingly work with others. But do they work as well as possible in teams? That is the concern of this book.

1.2 · Working in Teams: Barriers and Benefits

Why would anyone choose to do legal work with others? Let's ignore the first answer that may come to mind: because you will not have a choice. In practice you will likely be assigned to a client team, a trial team, a deal team, practice group, committee, or task force and be told to get to work. Let's go to a second scenario—assume that you have a choice about whether to assemble a group to do your work, perhaps because you are the lawyer responsible for accomplishing a complex task.

One of the barriers to working with others is attitude. Law practice management expert Jeffrey L. Nischwitz calls this the "I can do it myself" attitude: "It's not that I have to do it myself. It's just that if I do it myself I know that it's done, that it's done right, and that I can take it off the to-do list." (2007, p. 77). Lawyers may be more susceptible to the "I can do it myself" attitude problem than many professions. What was often rewarded before law school and what many feel got them into law school was individual hard work. The Anglo-American adversary system attracts, reinforces, and rewards an individualistic value of competition over cooperation or collaboration. Moreover, the adversary system frequently fails to recognize or reward the qualities of trust and interdependence that characterize successful teamwork.

As a result, until very recently, many Anglo-American legal educators largely rejected having students work together, and were unaware of the difference between collaborative and cooperative work. (Zimmerman, 1999). Because the phrase "cooperative and collaborative work" is frequently used as a synonym for group work or teamwork, it is important to understand the difference between these terms. "Cooperative work" describes situations where there is more individual accountability. An example of cooperative work is when multiple groups have separate but related objectives, such as separate defense teams representing different criminal defendants in a single trial. Each group is individually accountable, but would be more effective overall if they worked together. The educational parallel, "cooperative learning" involves students working together to individually master and be accountable for learning material through a group process.

In contrast, "collaborative work" describes situations where individuals work together toward a shared objective for which they are accountable as a group. The educational equivalent, "collaborative learning" asks students to work together toward a unified final product for which they are jointly accountable, usually in the form of a group grade (Id.). The main point of this reference to cooperative and collaborative pedagogy is that their common fundamental principles of classroom equality, shared authority, and student-centered learning are inherently at odds with traditional legal education, which has emphasized individual performance and achievement (Id.).

However, in the past thirty years, we have seen the supremacy of the adversary model of dispute resolution challenged by alternative modes of dispute resolution. These alternatives call for more cooperative and collaborative behavior, such as increased attention to negotiated settlements and mediation. At the same time, as we discuss below, we are seeing growing interest in group work in law school legal writing programs, clinics, and doctrinal courses. (Narko, Inglehart, & Zimmerman, 2003).

The increasing recognition that law is a business in addition to a profession has caused no end of lamentation. (Kronman, 1993). However, one positive dimension of this shift is the growing awareness that lawyers are expected to function effectively as part of client business teams, and in-house counsel positions are regularly part of senior management teams. These developments necessitate a shift in attitude away from the "I can do it myself" mentality. Moreover, as we discuss below, we see that fundamental principles of traditional legal education are being challenged more vigorously than ever before and are poised for change. We do not expect radical changes overnight. The conservative quality of the legal profession and legal educational institutions are likely to make this a gradual evolution of culture.

In addition to attitude, other barriers hinder effective teamwork. One barrier is the "free-rider" problem—where one member of a team fails to contribute effort, skill, or content comparable to others. It is highly frustrating to work hard, see progress, and realize that someone who did virtually nothing will receive equal credit for the fruits of your labor. Lawyers certainly appreciate this problem. Even the United States Supreme Court recognized it as one of the primary rationales for the doctrine of "attorney work product protection," which exempts from discovery and use at trial information prepared by or for the use of lawyers "in anticipation of litigation," because we do not want lazy lawyers leeching off the hard work of their colleagues and adversaries. (*Hickman v. Taylor*, 1947).

Another barrier to effective collaboration is having one person dominate others. The legal profession attracts many strong and intelligent individuals, puts them in a competitive environment, and teaches them to persuade. Unfortunately, not all of these individuals have developed interpersonal skills to the same degree that they have developed their analytical skills. Moreover, they frequently lack the self-awareness to realize their limitations.

When one member of a work group dominates, other members may find it easier just to shut down and let the dominator call the shots. However, this approach has several negative consequences. First, it can cause resentment and anger, especially if the entire group is held responsible for an inferior work product. Second, allowing the dominator to control can lead to the problem of **groupthink**. (Janis, 1983). Groupthink can occur when group members pressure others to conform to one particular view. Although creating agreement within a team is usually beneficial, groupthink produces negative results because it can lead to missed opportunities. Groupthink prevents the group from thinking creatively and searching for alternative solutions to problems. Moreover, groupthink short-circuits respect for individual participants in the group. Part of the value of a group process is that it employs the critical faculties of several individuals. This pressure of groupthink may come from an excessive enthusiasm for unity or because members of the group loathe conflict and do not know how to address it. One example of legal groupthink is illustrated in the movie classic *Twelve Angry Men*. In the movie, actor Henry Fonda's fellow jurors try to coerce him into going along with their initial decision to convict a young man of a crime without a full discussion of the evidence. The phenomenon of groupthink and methods of addressing it are discussed more in Chapter Four, where we show how conflict can actually be helpful in avoiding false confidence or excessive agreement among a group. Because teams can amplify individual problems with reasoning, we also discuss specific strategies for resolving decision-making problems in Chapter Five.

Another significant barrier to working collaboratively is that it is often more time-consuming than working individually. This is not universally true, but the perception that it is can be a significant barrier to effective teamwork. The fear of wasting time is not just personally aggravating—we've all been in ineffective meetings stewing over the waste of our valuable time—but in law, time is money. Clients may be reluctant to pay the billable hourly rate for each of two partners, two associates, and two paralegals as they strategize through pretrial and trial proceedings. If, however, the members of the legal team—lawyers, paralegals, administrative assistants, and other support staff—are crucial to meeting a client's goal, that expense is justified. This is the point of the book; the legal team can only work effectively with each other and the client or the client's team if they are willing to learn about and apply the best practices for working well collaboratively. Corporate clients, big and small, as well as large nonprofit and government organizations tend to be more familiar with the concepts we discuss in this book. They understand that an effective group or team can usually achieve bigger and better outcomes than even the most talented individual working alone. It is time for legal professionals to learn what the consumers of their services have known for a long time.

One of the tricks to effective teamwork is knowing when working collaboratively is not the best approach. Here are some of the situations in which it may be better to work individually than in a group:

- Time constraints are extremely tight—a decision must be made immediately.
- Distinct skills or knowledge is needed to do the work, and only one person has them.
- Tasks to be performed are unitary, non-divisible, and simple.
- Group members or the leader are unmotivated, untrained, or hostile to group work and the needs of the group.

(Lumsden, Lumsden & Wiethoff, 2010; Johnson & Johnson, 2006).

The downside of working collaboratively, whether from personality or situational problems, does not diminish its benefits. One benefit is expressed in the maxim "two heads are better than one," which has been validated empirically. (Cooke & Kernaghan, 1987). Because of the greater numbers involved in collaborative decision-making or problem-solving, the group has more information and experience to draw from. In addition, if team members are chosen strategically, the wider variety of skill sets and information-processing styles can generate and test ideas well beyond any one individual's capacity. Moreover, effective teams can be ideal when creative or "out-of-the-box" solutions are required. This is because teams have enhanced imaginative power and stimulating interactions among their members. A rather back-handed compliment to the effectiveness of the group process is the criminal law's concept of conspiracy. The law frequently treats criminal conspiracy with greater harshness than individual crimes because two or more criminals working in concert are thought to be more dangerous than one criminal working alone.

Another benefit of teamwork applies with special force in law school. Law students have long used study groups to learn legal concepts and practice their analytical and argumentation skills. However, as the movie *The Paper Chase* made clear, some of these groups work better than others—although we hope that no law student ever has to experience the self-destructive tendencies of some members of that infamous study group. Thus, one of our goals here is to help improve those under-performing groups by being better organized and by maximizing the strengths of the team dynamic while avoiding the pitfalls.

In conclusion, several individual benefits derive from successful teamwork. Research indicates that individuals experience strong psychological satisfaction from belonging to a productive team. Moreover, when decisions or solutions to problems are generated through a group process, group members tend to be more committed to the success of the group's solution. (Beebe & Masterson, 2003). Finally, when the group process is working well, individuals can develop a greater understanding of their personal and professional skills and weaknesses. Working with others provides a comparative context for observing how various members are viewed by the group and a reflection on how your contributions are viewed. If the team makes a practice of providing feedback to each other, the opportunities for professional and personal growth multiply. You can learn where your teammates find your contributions fall short and where they perceive your strengths. Of course, the degree to which you grow depends on your willingness to reflect and work on the feedback you receive from others. Conversely, the degree to which your teammates develop depends on the quality of the feedback you give them and their attitude toward that feedback. Chapter Two has suggestions for giving and receiving feedback.

1.3 · Our Focus and Approach to Teaching Collaborative Skills

As we have suggested, the central goal of this book is to increase the leadership ability of lawyers and other legal professionals in a deliberate and practical way. We want to help you develop your ability to create and participate in successful teams. This is a new topic for many law schools and lawyers. However, the time is right to add this subject to the list of the essential skills to teach. The winds of curricular change are blowing through legal education, with collaborative interpersonal skills at the top of the list of neglected lessons for legal professionals.

The serious movement began in the 1980s with a series of conferences and task forces (a prime example of a legal work group) that culminated in a 1992 publication, *Legal Education and Professional Development—An Educational Continuum: Report of the Task Force on Law Schools and the Profession: Narrowing the Gap*, commonly known as "the MacCrate Report." The MacCrate Report was the first major publication by the American Bar Association to exhort law schools to increase the number and variety of skills-based courses. It criticized the overwhelming dominance of doctrinal courses, which emphasize only the development of legal analytical skills and are taught primarily through the case-dominated "Socratic Method." The curricular renovation advocated by the MacCrate Report was followed by two major reports in 2007, *Best Practices for Legal Education* (Roy Stuckey et al.) and the Carnegie Foundation's report, *Educating Lawyers: Preparation for the Profession of Law* (William M. Sullivan et al.). Both the *Best Practices* and Carnegie Foundation reports encourage law schools to do more to help their students develop better work group and teamwork skills. The authors of *Best Practices* stated, "Students should be trained how to work in collaborative groups and be closely supervised to ensure these experiences reflect aspects of law practice collaboration and build on their collaborative skills." (Stuckey et al., p. 277). Researchers conducting the Law School Survey of Student Engagement ("LSSSE") agree, finding that:

> students benefit from opportunities to learn collaboratively. Whether studying one-on-one with another student to prepare for an exam or working with a group during class on a project, these interactions allow students to develop competencies that are essential to practice. Increasingly, law firms look for evidence of an ability to work well with others in hiring, compensation, and advancement decisions.

(2012 Annual Survey Results, p. 13).

Law school faculties are notoriously resistant to change, but there are signs that law professors are recognizing the need for training in collaborative skills. Faculty members who teach courses in legal writing and research and law school clinics have incorporated collaboration and cooperative learning techniques for some time. (Zimmerman, 1999). Some law school faculty members, especially ones who acknowledge the changing pedagogy in other professional fields, such as medical schools and M.B.A. programs, are encouraging their colleagues to incorporate more collaborative work into doctrinal courses. (Cassidy, 2012). Several law schools, such as Northwestern University, Georgetown University, Santa Clara University, and Harvard University, among others, have started to include training in cooperative and collaborative work in their curriculum. Northwestern University School of Law conducted extensive research with alumni, business, community, faculty and community leaders, finding that:

> In almost every environment that we explored, the ability to work effectively with others in teams or groups was considered absolutely necessary. The importance of teamwork was stressed by almost every person in our external focus groups. In practice, there are two primary models. In some cases, these teams or groups consist only of other lawyers, such as internal teams within law firms or in legal departments of other private, governmental, and non-profit organizations. Often, teams include a single lawyer or small numbers of lawyers working with clients and others who have different training and areas of expertise. Clients expect their lawyers to work effectively on such teams, contributing their skills to the common effort and learning from their fellow team members.

(Northwestern University School of Law, Plan 2008, p. 14).

As a result of this research and analysis, Northwestern expanded the core competencies for its graduates to include more than traditional legal analysis. Law graduates are also expected to learn communication, business, management, relationship, and leadership skills, all of which specifically emphasize the varied skills used to build high-performing legal and multi-disciplinary teams.

Despite the growing recognition of the need for training about group dynamics and professional teamwork in the law, we have seen no other legal texts devoted to this topic. There are, however, plenty of texts available on the general subject of teams, generally under the category of management skills. But among the millions of words we find little that is directly relevant to training lawyers, not because management theory is irrelevant to law but because many of these books are little more than sermons, setting forth parables about the value of teamwork in turning around dysfunctional organizations. They do not seem to focus on how to prevent dysfunction in the first place.

In this book we chose to focus on key insights and principles that law students, lawyers, judges, and other legal professionals can use and adapt to their own use. For this, we have turned to the best research-based knowledge developed in the fields of management, communication studies, and social psychology, as well as our own writing and experience. However, because we could not possibly summarize the entire amount of work available, we tried to be highly selective, winnowing the most relevant and practical information down to a manageable size for use by busy law students and lawyers. We provide an extensive list of excellent sources for further study in our list of references at the conclusion of the book. Finally, we interviewed many legal professionals from diverse practice areas and frequently use their stories—and our own experiences—to show how the concept or technique we discuss applies in the legal context.

Finally, we recognize that the practice of law is changing rapidly in part because of new modes of digital communication. Thus, throughout the book and more specifically in Chapter Six we give special emphasis to the growing reality of "virtual" teams, in which the participants interact remotely through a wide range of technology.

As with any other type of legal skill, such as writing or negotiating, some individuals will feel perfectly at home with collaborative work because they are naturally gifted at this type of communication. But everyone, even the naturally gifted, can improve the collaborative skills by building an understanding of the theory behind these processes. Everyone can also further develop their leadership teamwork skills with practice, and by critically reflecting on that practice. This is not a radically new mode of pedagogy, rather it is as old as the schools of legal advocacy in ancient Greece, where teachers would not only lecture or engage in the famous "Socratic" dialogue, immortalized by the philosopher Plato, but also would have students engage in mock legal debates. (Scallen, 2003). Today, this process of learning the theory behind legal skills, practicing them in different situations, and critically reflecting on their performance allows students, attorneys, or others, a higher degree of comfort and accomplishment.

The challenge is that working collaboratively can be hard. But in today's competitive markets there is no room for under-skilled or under-performing lawyers. A corporate in-house lawyer illustrated this point:

> Our company had an informal, relaxed community culture. We had a very good lawyer who was great when he was not under stress. [When he was under stress] he blew up at support staff, and me [his general counsel]. I worked really hard for years trying to help him. But people wanted to work less and less with him. I had to let him go.

The good news is that by improving your ability to work and lead effective legal teams you also improve your likelihood for professional success. But most important, learning to work well with others will improve your personal satisfaction as a legal professional. As one partner at a mid-size boutique law firm told us, "People notice your ability to work with others. Be aware of that. Don't be bashful about taking on group leadership tasks. If there is an opportunity to get leadership experience by volunteering for something, take it on." In this book, we aim to help you be more at ease and prepared to take on these team leadership roles.

Applications

1. Write down a list of some of your team experiences in legal and non-legal settings (school, work, friends, volunteer projects, public service, etc.).
2. What made these collaborative experiences effective?
3. What made them ineffective?
4. Who were the leaders who emerged and how did that occur?
5. Describe how you participated in the different groups.
6. Did you experience disagreements in any of those groups? If so, how did the group deal with the disagreement? How did you feel about it?
7. How did the groups develop or change over time?
8. How did the group members treat each other?
9. How organized or productive were the group meetings?
10. Was the group product better or worse than it would have been had you worked alone?
11. What did you learn from these experiences that you could apply in a professional environment?
12. What advice would you give to others about effective collaboration?

Chapter 2

Individual Groundwork for Working in Teams

2.1 · Motivation for Team Work

As suggested by the previous chapter, one of the biggest barriers to effective group work is staring at us in the mirror. Our own beliefs and attitudes about working with others on collaborative or cooperative projects are among the most significant determinants of how successful we are working in a team. Consider how many of the following fears or concerns arise as you think about working in a group.

- I do not like the possibility of being responsible and accountable for others' work product;
- I do not like the idea that others may take credit for my work;
- I do not know what makes groups work—either they do just work or they do not work;
- I have been in groups that were just painful to be around, not to mention complete failures;
- I have enough work to do without also having to learn all these "soft" skills and wasting time with other people's issues.

Many intelligent and accomplished individuals have these thoughts at some point, resulting in reactions that vary in degree from mild concern to high anxiety. These are the beliefs and attitudes that we have to tackle as individuals so that we can perform at our highest level, becoming a resource for the group rather than an obstacle to its success.

You may already be motivated by the research summarized in Chapter One, highlighting the demand of clients and legal employers for lawyers with strong interpersonal, cooperative, and collaborative skills. In case those authorities are insufficiently persuasive, however, here are a few more observations from an article that summarizes the efforts of innovative corporate law departments to improve the performance of their lawyers—individually and as a group:

- Talent development in law departments often starts with teamwork exercises, designed to capitalize on complementary skills to boost their team's overall effectiveness. For example, the law department of AlliedSignal … undertook the development and customization of training in many aspects of talent management, including team building.
- The law department of a major city invested in group leadership training in 1999. The workshop focused on teamwork as well as the supervisory skills senior lawyers needed to exhibit, such as feedback, communication and motivation.

(Morrison & Ashing, 2003, p. 7).

Nonetheless, if you have an aversion to working in small groups, your attitude may be grounded in past bad experiences and uncertainty about how to make teams work effectively. This chapter and the rest of the book are aimed at providing you with the confidence that comes from understanding how to do collaborative work effectively. The focus of this chapter, however, is on you. By learning about yourself, and how you differ from others, you can feel more comfortable and be more effective working on teams.

2.2 · Awareness of Personality, Preferences, and Difference: Yours and Theirs

Have you ever stopped to ask yourself:

- How do I see and think about the world?
- How do I perceive or absorb information?
- How do I organize and process that information?
- How do I come to conclusions or decisions?
- Where do I find energy and strength? In an external world of people, first-hand experience, and activity, or an internal world of ideas, theory, memory, and emotions?

And the final question:

• Can I confidently answer these questions about my preferences?

If you can easily answer these questions, congratulations! Because you understand your own preferences, you are better situated to recognize when others take different approaches. Thus, you have an opportunity to identify the approaches that complement your skills and preferences and use them when working collaboratively.

If you cannot confidently answer those questions about yourself, you may need to do some digging. Without knowing something about how you approach your work and deal with other people, it will be harder for you to appreciate and work with other group members' preferences and abilities. In addition, if you are not clear about your own preferences, you will be limited as you try to evaluate feedback from your group members and try to improve your collaborative skills. Moreover, if you lack this self-awareness, you are likely to fall into one of the biggest traps in working with others; you will assume that "great minds think alike," that everyone sees and thinks about the world as *you* do.

As we have suggested before, one of the best qualities of teamwork is that it can harness the full range of the group members' work preferences, abilities, and experience. Yet this potential may remain unrealized if individual members are unaware of how each individual works best, and are unable to engage their teammates' different preferences, interests, knowledge, skills, and experiences.

There are systematic methods of answering the questions raised above, ways to engage in self-analysis as well as to increase your understanding of the communication and problem-solving styles of other members of your group. The questions above come from the most widely used diagnostic instrument of different personality styles, the Myers-Briggs Type Indicator (MBTI™). The MBTI is not a diagnostic psychological test, that is, it is not intended to indicate abnormalities in reasoning, personality, or perception. Instead, the MBTI authors assume the person answering the MBTI questions is relatively mentally healthy, and has certain preferences that are clustered by personality type. An MBTI "personality type" describes a person's preferred ways of getting energized, approaching the world, thinking, and communicating, but does not measure or predict aptitude or ability.

The MBTI has been translated into sixteen languages and "is used by organizations of all stripes and most Fortune 500 companies." (Redding, 2008, p. 286). Lawyers who work heavily with corporate clients have discovered that clients may know their MBTI type and be curious about the MBTI types of those they work with. But it is not necessary to ask someone for their MBTI type to find the MBTI useful. Just understanding your own preferences can help you understand why you gravitate toward certain types of information, or why you find some people easier to work with than others. Understanding your own MBTI preferences can also alert you to aspects of your communication and problem-solving approaches that others may misinterpret or misunderstand. This kind of self-analysis is an important activity for any professional.

Thus, a growing number of lawyers and judges are using the MBTI personality instrument to increase their professional effectiveness. (Richard, 1993, 2008; Kennedy, 1998). Some law schools are using it in their career counseling. (Richard, 1993; Abrams, 2006; Redding, 2008). All of the authors of this book have taken the MBTI (two of us are certified to administer it) and have found it highly useful in our professional lives and personal relationships. One corporate attorney gave an example of how the MBTI could be used:

> We have an annual retreat for all lawyers in the company. We tried to build our EQ [emotional intelligence quotient]. We all took the MBTI and talked about group dynamics. Especially for less senior lawyers, it enabled us to talk about how lawyers should talk to corporate clients.

We briefly introduce the concept of the MBTI personality type here as one tool that can assist you in working collaboratively. Using the MBTI can help you understand and appreciate different communication and decision-making styles, and there are many studies about the implications of MBTI and personality types for different work environments. If you are reading this text as part of your coursework, your professor may arrange for you to take the MBTI or a different tool for evaluating your work preferences and communication style. If you are studying this book on your own, you can find a certified practitioner to administer the MBTI through the Association for Psychological Type International (www.aptinternational.org), or through the Center for the Application of Psychological Type (www.capt.org). We strongly recommend that you use a certified practitioner to administer the MBTI and help you interpret the results.

There is a great deal of misinformation about the MBTI. So-called "personality tests" allegedly based on the MBTI are more confusing than helpful. We will discuss the concerns that some critics have raised about the MBTI in greater detail after we explain what it is and the theory behind it, but we need to emphasize a few points up front. The study of human personality is one of the most controversial areas of contemporary psychology. There are many approaches to studying and describing personality "traits" or "types," and the topic far exceeds the scope of this book. However, we believe it is important to develop "working hypotheses" concerning your own preferences about decision-making and communication and how they may differ from those of others if you want to work well with others.

The MBTI is just one approach of many used to understand differences in the way people approach and communicate about their work. However, it is one of the best known and most widely used, so we have chosen to discuss it here. **But please be aware of the following caveats in our discussion of the MBTI.** First, any certified administrator of the MBTI will agree that a person's preferences or observed behavior can—and does—change over time and context. So it is misleading to suggest that the various MBTI "types" are offered or presented as fixed "boxes" to use to categorize or sort yourself and others. Virtually all contemporary theorists—including certified MBTI users—accept the dynamic quality of personality. (Lucas & Donnellan, 2009). Thus, they must acknowledge that any effort to "predict" someone's "personality" with confidence is a futile and misleading exercise. As a result, individuals who are certified to use the MBTI may not, under the terms of their certification, ethically use the tool for purposes of selection. (Myers, 1998). Critics may point to abuses of the MBTI, but that does not mean the tool is illegitimate or useless. Second, thoughtful users of the MBTI acknowledge that there is wide disagreement among psychologists about whether personality "traits" or "types" can be defined; there is even disagreement about what to call various facets of personality—traits, types, factors, domains, dimensions, preferences, etc. Third, of the personality factors that have been defined, there is disagreement over which ones matter to being an effective professional. In addition to the MBTI types discussed below, various psychologists stress the importance of "emotional stability," "resilience," and "empathy," among other personal qualities for professional success.

No credible user suggests that the MBTI provides a complete picture of an individual's "personality." Moreover, we do not mean to dismiss the potential importance of other personal factors by focusing on those emphasized by the MBTI. We do conclude that the preferences revealed by the MBTI provide a useful introductory framework for understanding different modes of thinking and communicating among members of legal groups or teams. Understanding potential differences can help teams maximize their strengths in accomplishing their tasks and minimize the relationship conflicts they experience. But the key to using the MBTI successfully is to realize that it is not a personality "test" that helps you categorize yourself or others. When administered and explained appropriately, the MBTI provides a tool for understanding and adapting to difference, while acknowledging that preferences are fluid. The MBTI will help you develop working hypotheses about how to adapt to the preferences of others; it does not promise and cannot deliver fixed or permanent answers about human personality. Even with its limitations, the MBTI has proven helpful to a wide range of legal professionals and their clients, so it is worth discussing here. However, like all good lawyers, we will present the "other side" and its criticism of the MBTI in more detail after the following explanation of the theory and the MBTI types.

The MBTI is based on psychotherapist Carl Jung's theories about personality difference among healthy persons along four dimensions: their preferences for

(1) obtaining mental energy,
(2) gathering information,
(3) making decisions, and
(4) dealing with their environments.

The name of the instrument comes from its original creators, Katharine Cook Briggs and Isabel Briggs Myers, who designed the first Type Indicator, a questionnaire containing a series of dichotomies (either/or questions) asking about an individual's preferences along those four dimensions. The results of the MBTI are reported as scores that indicate a person's preferences along four different dimensions, represented by their initials:

- Extraversion or Introversion (E or I)
- Sensing or iNtuition (S or N) (the MBTI uses capital "N" because the "I" was already taken by "Introversion")
- Thinking or Feeling (T or F)
- Judging or Perceiving (J or P)

The usual process for taking the MBTI involves learning about the different personality type preferences, completing the full type indicator questionnaire, engaging in further self-assessment, and participating in a feedback session with exercises to illustrate the differences between your self-identified type and the types of others. Here we can only describe each dimension of type briefly and suggest how it applies to lawyers.

Extraversion versus Introversion. This dimension describes how an individual interacts with two worlds: the external world of people, physical environments, and events or conditions, and the internal world of thoughts, feelings, and sensations. Those who gravitate toward the Extraversion end of the scale focus on and are energized by the world around them. Extraverted types tend to have large networks of social contacts, enjoy action-filled interactions, and think aloud. They enjoy tossing ideas around with others, and react easily to new ideas being tossed at them. They do not like silence, and will speak to fill it up. After a day of meetings, the Extravert wants to go to dinner or another social event to continue the interaction with her colleagues.

In contrast, Introverts focus within, on their thoughts and mental impressions. It is important to note several common misunderstandings and misperceptions about introverts:

- Introverts are not necessarily shy and can be just as passionate and excited about ideas as extraverts, but they react to people, the environment, and communication differently.
- Introverts can enjoy the company of other people as much as Extraverts, but often prefer to take those interactions in smaller, shorter doses.
- Introverts tend to prefer one-on-one interactions, solitary activities (such as reading), and thinking about issues before speaking about them. When Introverts speak, they want to share their complete train of thought without interruption. (Cain 2012; Myers, 1998).

After a day of meetings, an Introvert likely prefers to have some down time, when he can be alone or with one or two people with whom he feels very comfortable, before he meets with colleagues for dinner. The Introvert may also prefer dining with just one or two colleagues, as opposed to a large group.

Sensing versus Intuition. The second dimension describes how a person absorbs information about the world. Those toward the Sensing end of the scale take in the world by focusing on what they can actually see, hear, or touch. They gravitate toward concrete details or facts. People with Sensing type preferences value past experience because it can be collected, categorized, quantified, and described. Sensing types are "data-driven"; they thrive on precision and accuracy. Their communication style tends to be very literal and factual. They are grounded in the here and now, the practical and useful. At the other end of the scale, those with an Intuition preference take a "Big Picture" view of the world. For them, facts are there to be interpreted, to be examined for overarching patterns or ultimate meaning. They do not like to get bogged down in detail. They see information as a springboard to possibilities and future issues. Their communication style has a narrative, story-telling quality.

Thinking versus Feeling. The third dimension describes the way in which people evaluate information and make decisions. As discussed below, this is an area in which legal professionals have differed significantly from the general population. The Thinking type values logical decision-making, using facts to deduce conclusions from principles or rules regardless of the impact of those decisions. Those with Thinking preferences evaluate information with a degree of personal detachment; they see themselves as objective. In communicating with others, Thinking types appear highly critical, challenging the reasoning of others, searching for evidence behind the others' statements, and constantly asking: "Why?"

In contrast to someone with a Thinking preference, a person with a Feeling preference evaluates information and makes decisions through the prism of his values and his relationships with others. Feeling types are not inherently illogical; they just do not rely on logic alone. Feeling types care about the consequences of their decisions on others and would be willing to modify the decision to mitigate negative consequences. Feeling types prefer harmony and tend to take conflict personally. A common misconception is that someone with a Feeling preference is highly emotional. Carl Jung, however, did not describe the Feeling type as emotional. A more accurate interpretation of his description would be "valuing." (Richard, 1993, p. 76).

Judging versus Perceiving. As with the other MBTI personality types, the labels can be misleading. Contrary to how it sounds, the final dimension is not about being judgmental or observant; the Judging-Perceiving scale describes how individuals generally prefer to organize their lives. The Judging type prefers a planned, systematic, and orderly life. They are decisive and do not second-guess their decisions. The Judging types like closure and usually seek to get a project or decision finished as efficiently as possible. They are less comfortable with ambiguity, uncertainty, or interruptions. Those with a Judging preference like to have control over their environment, are methodical planners, and are usually very punctual.

Those with a preference for Perceiving tend to be more flexible, spontaneous, and informal. Perceiving types like to think about all possibilities and keep their options open. They are not comfortable ruling out possible conclusions and will not do so unless they have to. Perceiving types tolerate ambiguity and uncertainty well. They like to work on a variety of projects at once. Not surprisingly, Perceiving types have problems with procrastination and punctuality. But they are responsive to deadlines, which force them to focus on one particular outcome.

Table 2.1 · The Lawyer Types

Type Preferences of Lawyers

Extraversion	vs.	Introversion
43%		57%
Sensing	vs.	Intuition
43%		57%
Thinking	vs.	Feeling
78%		22%
Judging	vs.	Perceiving
63%		37%

(Richard, 1993). © ABA Journal, Dr. Larry Richard. Used by Permission.

Dr. Larry Richard is a lawyer and psychologist who directs the Leadership & Organization Development Practice Group of Hildebrandt International, a professional services firm specializing in the development of legal professionals. Around 1992, he collected data from over 3,000 lawyers throughout the U.S. who had completed the MBTI. He found some stark differences among lawyers and the general population, especially on certain scales. For example, in the general population, about 75% describe themselves as extraverted, with no significant difference between genders. Lawyers, in contrast, were more introverted than the general population and there *was* a difference between genders. In Richard's sample of 3,000, only 41% of the male lawyers described themselves as extraverted, while 49% of women lawyers described themselves that way. (Richard, 1993).

The difference between extraverts and introverts can cause communication and personal misunderstandings. An extravert may be frustrated if an introvert does not immediately fire back with a verbal response in their conversations. The extravert may also not understand why the introvert is not talking, assuming that he is lazy, disinterested, or inept. The introvert may feel threatened, pressured, or rushed by an extravert to respond too quickly. Some lawyers who have learned about their own type and others' preferences have learned to adjust their communication style to suit the person they are trying to influence. An introvert may need to learn to speak up more often and more quickly to address an extravert's preference for a quick response. On the other hand, the extravert may need to work on her listening skills. As we discuss below, developing effective listening skills facilitates working collaboratively. Later in this chapter we talk more about how to listen effectively.

In Richard's study about lawyers and MBTI types, the Sensing-Intuition dimension also differed for lawyers compared to the general population. Nationally, the majority of those taking the MBTI describe themselves as sensing (about 70%). In contrast, the majority of lawyers taking the MBTI (about 57%) described a preference for intuition with no significant difference between genders. The differences on this scale within Richard's sample of lawyers showed up in choice of legal specialty. Lawyers with a sensing preference "choose real estate, tax and general practice, while a greater number of intuitive types chose criminal, litigation and labor law." (Richard, 1993, p. 76).

The differences between sensing and intuition preferences can create unproductive interpersonal conflict when they are not understood. The sensing type may resent what he perceives as carelessness with the facts. And those with a preference for intuition may resent the sensing type's obsession with detail, missing the forest for the trees. Here is one obvious example where appreciating difference in personality types can improve collaborative work. Having some members with sensing preferences and others with intuition preferences on a team could be extremely helpful because the different types will focus on different things, bringing a more complete analysis to any problem. A small law firm partner told us about the partner's case management approach that reflects this approach:

> Jane and Joe are partners in a small law office. They divide their cases between the two of them, then each divides their cases between their two associates so that each associate works with each partner. Jane and Joe have very different management styles. Jane is the trial lawyer and a self-described micro manager (the details). Joe does the appellate work and has much more of a hands-off style of supervision (big picture/long range). However, when cases approach critical junctures like summary judgment, trial, and oral argument, all partners and associates gather in the conference room to strategize, present and moot, and generally gather and maximize their complementary strengths for the case.

If those with sensing and intuition preferences fail to appreciate their differences, however, that potential advantage can become a cause of communication failure, animosity, and, ultimately, ineffectiveness.

Richard's study further showed that the Thinking-Feeling dimension also sets lawyers apart from the general U.S. population. While the general population divides about equally into Thinking and Feeling types, 78% of lawyers describe themselves as thinkers. (Richard, 1993). This scale also reveals a gender difference. In the general population, approximately 60% of men describe themselves as Thinking types, while about 35% of women describe themselves as Thinking. When looking at just the sample of lawyers, those figures rise to 81% of male lawyers preferring Thinking and 66% of women lawyers identifying they have a Thinking preference. (Richard, 1993). However, when looking at gender differences on the MBTI, one has to beware of cultural norms that may encourage women to express Feeling preferences. Moreover, Richard more recently reported that, although the statistics for the other scales have been remarkably stable for lawyers since his 1993 study, the number of lawyers reporting a preference for Feeling has increased recently for both men and women, which he speculates is due to the influx of "Gen Y," younger lawyers who "are more interpersonal, more interested in collegiality, relationships, climate, etc." (Richard, 2007). Nevertheless, among lawyers, those with Thinking preferences still dominate over those with Feeling preferences.

As a result of the personality differences, the same possibility for unproductive conflict in communication exists between those with Thinking or Feeling preferences. The Thinking type assumes that everyone uses the same analytical and depersonalized approach to problem-solving that he uses. The Thinking person does not take conflict personally, but the Feeling person may. To a lawyer with Thinking preferences, the Feeling lawyer can seem naïve or irrational; to a Feeling lawyer, the Thinking lawyer may appear insensitive, cold, and confrontational. Those with Thinking and Feeling preferences can make significant strides in improving their collaborative efforts if they are willing to recognize others' different communication styles and adjust accordingly. For a lawyer with a Thinking preference, this means avoiding a "cross-examination" style of probing for information. When working with a Feeling lawyer or client, it also helps a lawyer with a Thinking preference to pay sincere attention to relational aspects at the outset of communication, such as by asking about family and social activities even if such considerations seem irrelevant to the discussion. Establishing this common ground may make it possible for clients, colleagues, or opposing counsel with Feeling preferences to listen and accept the logic of Thinking types as they analyze a problem together.

In contrast, Feeling types can learn to recognize the critical tone of Thinking types and work to realize that the criticism is not intended as a personal slight, but rather as an attempt to improve the problem-solving process. Finally, as much as logical analysis is prized in law school and the legal profession, the best lawyers know that cases and transactions do not live or die by logic alone. A perfectly "rational" proposed solution to a legal problem may be a potential disaster if it ignores the values of the individuals who are responsible for making a decision or who are responsible for implementing a solution successfully. A large firm managing partner described his style that reflects this approach:

> Do not dictate to team members. Discuss, explain, and build on all points. Thus, even if you have the final say, an authoritative role, or most of the expertise, it is in your best interest to explain all: why, changes, and actions. Have humility and get into conversations.

Another lawyer illustrated the importance of being visibly valued by his supervisor. Wayne, a senior associate with a large national law firm, works with a senior attorney who is a great lawyer. "He is hard working, nice, and is someone others like to work with." This mentor shows that he values his working relationship with Wayne; as Wayne stated, "He sees that I can be much more successful, and he wants me to get there." The power of this communication and relationship is huge:

> If [the senior attorney] asks me to do anything, I will do it. I won't do it for everyone, but I will want to be a team player for him, because I have a personal relationship with him. He's a great attorney. He's very personable. He is a pleasure to work with. There are a lot of assholes you have to work with. But you do things because of the relationship. I have yet to say "no" to this guy because of my relationship with him.

Thus, Thinking types would do well to listen to and appreciate the relationship values of Feeling types, just as Feeling types may benefit from testing any solution against the Thinking type's rigorous analysis.

The final scale, Judging versus Perceiving, also sets lawyers apart from the general population, but to a lesser degree. The general population divides equally into Judging and Perceiving preferences. Among lawyers, however, about 63% describe themselves as Judging types while 37% report a Perceiving preference. (Richard, 1993). This scale shows no strong gender bias the way the Thinking-Feeling scale did, either among the general population or among lawyers, although a slightly higher percentage of women lawyers reported a Judging preference than male lawyers (67% for women versus 61% for men).

Understanding the difference between the Judging and Perceiving preferences can go a long way toward preventing personal conflict. A large percentage of the difference here has to do with the timing of work and decisions; the

Judging type prefers to get things done sooner, while the Perceiving type prefers to do things later. Anxiety arises on both sides. The Perceiving type feels pushed and rushed while the Judging type fears that the work will not get done or will be done sloppily at the last minute. These types need to understand that the other is not deliberately trying to drive the other crazy with their work habits. They need to reach a negotiated compromise on how and when the project will be accomplished. In doing so, these types need to develop a strong amount of trust and respect for the other—the Judging type has to know that the Perceiving type will get the job done and done well. The Perceiving type has to honor the Judging type's need for measurable progress and organization. It is not easy, but it can be done.

One example of the importance of recognizing the difference between Judging and Perceiving preferences is in the existence of this book, which is a tribute to the compromises among the authors, one of whom has a strong Perceiving preference. This author would prefer to keep researching, writing, and re-writing endlessly, and needed the structure and deadlines provided and kindly enforced by the two other authors, who have strong Judging preferences.

When an individual takes the MBTI, she receives a final result of four letters that, together, describe the individual's composite psychological type. Richard found that of the 16 possible types more than half of all lawyers are represented by just four types: ISTJ (Introvert, Sensing, Thinking, and Judging), ESTJ (Extravert, Sensing, Thinking, and Judging), INTJ (Introvert, Intuition, Thinking, and Judging), and ENTP (Extravert, Intuition, Thinking, and Perceiving). (Richard, 1993, p. 77). Note the dominance of the "TJ" (Thinking-Judging) pair, describing a "no-nonsense, logical, bottom-line approach." (Id.). Whether the "TJ" pair is a dominant preference for lawyers or not, it is important to remember that the Myers-Briggs Type Indicator describes fifteen other personality types and every single one of them is represented in the legal profession. (Richard, 1993).

It is also vital to remember that the dominance of the Thinking-Judging preferences in law does not necessarily apply to the wide range of individual clients, representatives of government agencies, and members of the general public with whom lawyers and other legal professionals work. One unnamed local bar publication published a "top ten" list of rules for communicating with clients. "Poor communication" has consistently been one of the top complaints clients have about their lawyers, producing the largest number of complaints to lawyer disciplinary boards. However, one of the rules about communicating with clients was wrong. It said that your personality type did not matter, and, the only personality type that matters is the audience's type. Although it is important to focus on the listener's personality type to communicate and work effectively, the difficulty with this rule is you may not be able to determine that person's preferences. Nevertheless, being aware of your own preferences allows you to make sure that you are not just playing to one type—your own. Then, you can develop a strategy. To do so, remember to ask others how *they* prefer to work and communicate:

- Would they rather meet in person or by telephone, or would e-mail, texting, or instant messaging work best for them?
- Do they prefer to have time to think about the options or would they like to discuss them together with you, right now?
- Would they like to break the project into parts and develop a schedule right now, or would they prefer to study the problem and think about the possibilities for a while before developing a work plan?
- What kind of data or facts do they think the group needs to collect before members of the group will be ready to make a decision?

The time spent on this basic audience analysis will pay off extraordinarily well in terms of having better working relationships. It is also common for MBTI practitioners to publicly identify their types so you can gain some insight into their perspective and communication styles. In that spirit, here are the verified MBTI types of your authors: Eileen Scallen is an INFP (Introvert, Intuitive, Feeling, and Perceiving); Cliff Zimmerman is an ISTJ (Introvert, Sensing, Thinking, and Judging); and Sophie Sparrow is an ESFJ (Extravert, Sensing, Feeling, and Judging).

The MBTI is not the only way to learn about your communication, learning, and problem-solving styles and preferences. We use it, however, to illustrate the kind of self-analysis that can lead to better working relationships with other team members. The MBTI, as well as the personality trait theory on which it is based, has its critics. (Redding, 2008; Paul, 2004). Some of the critiques of the MBTI are based on a misunderstanding of the role of a personality inventory such as the MBTI. The MBTI is not intended to and cannot predict which personality types will receive the highest grades in law school or which types will make the most money as practicing lawyers. The lack of predictive power does not make the MBTI useless. The law is filled with examples of descriptive taxonomies and heuristics that have proven useful through the years. We do not dismiss them, even though they do not claim scientific "predictive" significance.

Some critics also question the descriptive reliability and validity of the sixteen personality "types" recognized by the MBTI. This critique may have some merit, in that it has not been proven that there are only sixteen personality types among humans. Additional tools, such as the MBTI Step II, can add a layer of nuance to the MBTI self-analysis. For example, when Professor Eileen

Scallen took the MBTI Step II (Form M) instrument, she received results indicating that she is a "Gregarious, Logical, Planful INFP." Scallen reports that this more detailed description of her "type" is more accurate, because she has developed some of her decision-making preferences over time to the point where she is equally comfortable with both. For example, she has equally strong preferences for logical analysis (not surprising given her legal training and academic career) and for making decisions consistent with her values and relationships with others. In other words, this type description fits her better.

One "personality inventory" is unlikely to capture the essence or all of the nuances of any particular person, which is good. But critiques of the MBTI that rest on "snapshot" or summary descriptions of the various types and then compare the MBTI to newspaper horoscopes discredit themselves with their own lack of intellectual rigor. The critics may shake their heads and wonder why the MBTI has been so popular, but the MBTI has proven helpful to a wide variety of sophisticated users in professional settings. It seems doubtful that so many Fortune 500 companies, professional sports teams, and the U.S. Naval Academy among other users, would invest as much time and money on a method of self-analysis that is practically worthless, as some critics claim the MBTI is. (Redding, 2008; Paul, 2004). We take a more pragmatic, lawyerly approach to the MBTI—understand its limitations, and use it thoughtfully as one tool to help improve your ability to appreciate the differences in the way you and others approach, perceive, think, and talk about your work and world.

Let's reframe this issue even more pragmatically. You undoubtedly have your preferred answers to the questions at the beginning of this section, but recognizing your preferences may be insufficient to successful collaboration. We rarely think about asking others these questions about *their* work, decision-making, and communication preferences. Their answers can provide extremely helpful information. Others' preferences may suggest ground rules that will remove some of the barriers to misunderstanding and unnecessary conflict. In addition, if you can honor others' preferences while asking others for what you need to work most effectively, you are more likely to accomplish the team's goals. This combination of self-understanding and appreciating colleagues' differences provides your group with the chance for greater satisfaction and productivity. Cliff Zimmerman reports that, as Dean of Students at Northwestern Law, he often talks with students about change and adaptation because he understands the personal growth that can take place. Once you know your baseline preferences, you can work on building flexibility by taking on challenges that require using approaches you do not prefer. For example, Zimmerman's type, ISTJ (Introvert, Sensing, Thinking, and Judging), is not an obvious fit for a Dean of Students, who must engage with faculty colleagues, students, and alumni on a virtually nonstop basis. Someone with a Feeling preference might appear to be more effective in a position where sensitivity to building relationships is central to the daily job. But Zimmerman has found the work to be enormously rewarding. By being aware of his preferences, he then makes sure that he gets some quiet time to recharge after a long day perhaps by running alone, then he is far more comfortable and productive in his job than one might expect.

2.3 · Effective Listening: Not as Easy as It Sounds

"Listening is as powerful a means of communication and influence as to talk well."
—John Marshall, first Chief Justice of the United States Supreme Court

In *The Lost Art of Listening*, Michael P. Nichols captures a fundamental problem in many people's lives:

> Contemporary pressures have, regrettably, shrunk our attention spans and impoverished the quality of listening in our lives.... Running to and from our many obligations, we get a lot of practice in not listening....
>
> We've gained unparalleled access to information and lost something very important. We've lost the habit of concentrating our attention. From pop music at the gym to commercials on TV and radio we're bombarded with so much noise that we've become experts at tuning things out. If a television show doesn't grab our attention in the first two minutes, we change the channel; if we're listening to someone who doesn't get right to something we're interested in, we tune out.

(Nichols, 2009, p. 2). It is astounding that we work hard at *not* listening and have learned how to tune out. In contrast, we spend very little time learning and practicing to listen better. And yet, high-level executives estimate that approximately two-thirds of their communication time is spent listening. (Steil, 1997).

The lack of attention to listening is unfortunate, because we have many different reasons to listen well. For example, we listen for pleasure (music, theatre, television), to build social connections (conversation with friends and family), to obtain information (the weather report, the news, airport gate change announcements), or to understand (another's feelings, an event personally observed, or an event experienced by another). To listen well "sounds" deceptively simple, but poor listening skills are the root of so many unnecessary conflicts, damaged relationships, and unsuccessful work projects. One of the senior in-house attorneys we spoke to pointed out that, as lawyers, we are generally not very good listeners. She further stated that she had worked with many lawyers "who were unwilling to listen to non-lawyers. The ones who didn't listen did not last at the company." She continued to explain how listening well is more than just physically hearing what is said. "Some lawyers are unwilling to unpack what the meeting seemed to be about. They are unwilling to try to understand what was going on, rather than just being frustrated."

While it is obvious that listening is an essential skill for any lawyer, it is worth thinking about all of listening's benefits to motivate yourself to do the hard work necessary to become a better listener. An effective listener, who can make another person feel heard, acknowledged, and understood, is more likely to convince another person to keep an open mind and more likely to consider the listener's position. The psychological principle of reciprocity, that we tend to treat others as we feel they have treated us, is powerful. (Cialdini, 2006). If we listen with care and can accurately summarize and repeat another person's perspective or argument, that person is more likely to accept our analysis of that perspective or argument. Similarly, if we are willing to listen attentively to someone's critique of our positions, we are in a better position to spot the problems with our arguments.

Listening carefully allows participants to find the common ground that will allow them to work through disagreements and resolve problems together. Moreover, as is discussed in greater depth below, listening well frequently means paying attention to a speaker's nonverbal as well as verbal messages. Being an effective listener can help reveal underlying issues, ones not explicitly expressed, such as issues of trust, anger, resentment, or frustration. Frequently, these deeper issues must be acknowledged and addressed before you can make progress on more surface issues, such as allocating work assignments, determining deadlines for completing tasks, or discussing work performance. Here is an example from Cora, a real estate attorney, who spoke with us.

> Cora tries to really listen to her clients and understand their deep underlying and often-unacknowledged concerns. She noted that for many clients, buying a home is one of their biggest financial decisions. As a result, emotions are high. "Buying a home has people thinking about home, family; it taps into their primary needs." When things don't work well, such as when a client is distraught at seeing a seller's cigarette butts and dirty dishes just before to the final contract is

signed, Cora uses a lot of encouraging and echoing words. She pointed out that sometimes people need to be heard. Cora will take the time to talk to her client alone and to empathize with her anger and frustration. "I hear it was a frustrating experience. You want to bring up your babies in this home. You want this to be the perfect home. It's upsetting to see your dream home like this." Eventually, Cora was able to close the deal; "I remained compassionate."

Table 2.2 contrasts the habits and techniques that distinguish weaker from stronger listeners. While any one individual might demonstrate qualities from both columns in varying degrees, the best way to improve your listening skills is to emulate the best practices of effective listeners.

Table 2.2 · Habits of Weak Listeners versus Effective Listeners

The Weak Listener	The Effective Listener
Daydreams or drifts off, especially if the subject is dry or the speaker's delivery is monotone.	Does not let the speaker or topic's limitations defeat the listener's purpose for listening; works to gather the relevant information.
Listener allows herself to be distracted, such as by a smart phone or similar tool, e-mail, computer games, doodling, reading material, or visual aids.	Resists, or if necessary, removes all potential distractions, electronic or otherwise, from the environment (e.g., leaves the smart phone in the briefcase!).
Takes in only the verbal content.	Watches the speaker's nonverbal conduct to help interpret the speaker's message—facial expressions, tone of voice, posture, hands, fidgeting, body movements, or body position, level of eye contact.
Takes notes like a court reporter, trying to record the speaker's every word.	Adjusts the note-taking strategy to the situation. For example, when seeking information, the listener will focus on recording the central ideas. When in a situation where there is interpersonal conflict, the listener may take no notes. If a record is necessary, the listener has someone else take notes or records the conversation in some other fashion or immediately after.

The Weak Listener	The Effective Listener
Develops instant rebuttal and counterarguments to the speaker's points before hearing the speaker's entire case. Jumps into speaking, sometimes interrupting the other speaker.	Waits for the speaker to finish before evaluating and responding. During the speaker's time, the listener focuses on mentally understanding, organizing, and summarizing the speaker's ideas. Leaves a few moments of silence to see if the speaker has more to say before responding.
Does not practice listening to complex or difficult material, choosing only "easy listening": familiar, shallow, noncontroversial content and speakers with whom the listener already agrees.	Practices listening skills, balancing "easy listening" with more difficult subjects and speakers (especially speakers with whom the listener expects to disagree).
"Shuts down" or stops listening when the speaker uses offensive language or "buzz" words and phrases that trigger strong emotions in the listener.	Recognizes the emotional response to the speaker's language, but continues to look for the speaker's central idea and supporting points. Will remember the purpose for listening and will not be deterred by the speaker's choices. Will realize that the speaker may not have intended to be offensive and will distinguish the emotion triggered by the speaker from the substance. Will clarify with questions or debrief with others later.
Assumes he accurately understood everything the speaker said.	Asks questions to clarify the speaker's terms and ideas. Reflects and tests comprehension by occasionally paraphrasing the speaker's verbal and nonverbal messages: "Let me make sure I understood what you said," "Sounds like you are saying...."
Has a "poker face." Makes no physical or vocal response to the speaker. Uses counterproductive body language, such as arms crossed over chest, avoids eye contact.	Encourages the speaker by providing responsive nonverbal conduct, such as leaning forward toward the speaker, maintaining eye contact, and nodding. Also uses verbal encouragement, such as "Mmmhmm"; "I see" "Oh?" "Sure, yes, go on" "Can you say more about that?" "You sound angry about...."

Rachel, who works for a large public agency, summarizes the importance of listening intentionally and how this helps her in the workplace. She has learned how important it is to defer to people with expertise and ask for help early on. Rachel noted that "letting people educate you, letting them tell you what they know and making sure you understand it" allowed her to gain deeper understanding of the bigger strategic picture of the agency, realize whom she needed to talk to, and recognize complexities within the agency. Listening allows her to add value to the agency and colleagues. "I often don't know anything that will be helpful with others' projects. But because I have gone around and learned about what many people do at the agency, I can often connect people to other people who can help. In that way, I can still offer something of value."

2.4 · Giving and Receiving Feedback

Understanding how to give and take feedback necessarily follows from the previous section on listening. There is no way to give meaningful feedback to others in your team if you have not practiced the effective listening skills described earlier. And, of course, you cannot use the feedback you receive if you do not listen to it with an open mind. Since we already emphasized listening skills, this section focuses on giving and internally processing feedback. While Chapter Four more fully addresses managing conflict, giving and receiving feedback when done correctly also manages conflict by helping to avoid destructive conflict.

As with the process of listening, giving and absorbing feedback is far more difficult than it seems. Unlike listening, however, feedback has an emotional tone. Consider the following experience we heard from a law professor who teaches a clinic that uses both law students and non-law students as investigators:

> Early on the students did not talk about how to give feedback. The law students presented their legal work to the non-law students. The non-law students, not understanding the legal process and its limitations, delivered feedback that was heavily critical and negative. They thought they were being constructive, but the law students took it personally and were in tears.

Another word for feedback is criticism, which has an inherently negative connotation. As is obvious from the example, it does not help much to call it constructive criticism. But criticism need not be negative. At its essence, criticism is a process of describing, analyzing, and evaluating a performance. The evaluation itself can ultimately be positive, negative, or mixed. Although feedback and evaluation are obviously related, we see them as separate steps in a process. Being prepared and willing to give and receive feedback are individual skills necessary to help you and the other members of your group adjust your performance as you engage in your tasks. Although you may also incorporate intermediate forms of evaluation as a project evolves, more of your time may be spent affirming helpful conduct and discouraging unhelpful or counterproductive behavior. Some individuals are especially reticent when it comes to giving or taking feedback; we address particularly challenging group behaviors in Chapter Four. Here, we introduce best practices for giving and taking feedback in less antagonistic situations.

The goal of effective feedback is to change an individual's behavior. No amount of the highest quality feedback is likely to change a person's underlying personality or character. Whether we are talking about giving or receiving effective feedback, the central challenge is the same, individuals tend to be highly protective of their own self-conception. The self-concept is a composite of emotionally charged images of intelligence, achievements, and self-worth ranging from the most abstract philosophies, such as, "I am a conservative," to the most specific, "I always use good grammar." A person builds a conception of himself over time, deeply embedding that self-conception and making it highly resistant to change. We all have self-concepts we jealously guard, whether we appear outwardly self-confident or insecure.

To use an example, one of the authors occasionally listens to law professors talk about the student evaluations they have received over time. In listening to these colleagues, Scallen reports that she gets glimpses of their self-concepts. Often, the colleagues she admires the most are highly self-critical. These colleagues will talk at great length about some negative student evaluation, such as how much it hurt to read. When she asks them how the evaluations were on the whole, the response is almost always the same: they shrug it off and say, "oh, fine, but then there was this one...." This response suggests that overall the colleague's student evaluations were great, but the colleague chose to focus on a few negative ones. The painful evaluations become the focus in part because those comments reinforce the colleague's conception about his ability. For contrast, Scallen has sometimes asked her more self-confident colleagues about their student evaluations. Some tell her that they do not bother to read them. They assume that their teaching is excellent; if some students don't recognize that, then that reflects poorly on the student, not the professor. Giving or receiving effective feedback, feedback that reinforces desired performance and directs changes to unsatisfactory performance, means recognizing the roadblock of individual self-concept.

One of the attorneys we spoke to illustrated how she was able to identify her self-concept, and the hurdle that it was presenting for her. Early on in her practice, Cora viewed herself as someone who was very good at explaining things to people she worked with. Cora assumed that people would know what she meant, even if she did not provide all the details. "At first I assumed that if I asked someone to go from A to Z that they knew all the steps in between. But now I know that I often need to spell out the *whole* alphabet." Cora acknowledged that making the change was difficult: "Giving detailed directions without being a nag is challenging." Now she realizes that it is hard to give too much direction.

2.4.1 · Guidelines for Giving Effective Feedback

Some advice on giving helpful feedback is pretty straightforward, however like a lot of advice it is easier to give than to do.

- Good feedback **is specific.** The speaker uses actual examples of the desired or undesirable behavior.
- Good feedback **emphasizes description and analysis.** It focuses on observable actions, work product, and outcomes. Effective feedback avoids using evaluative conclusions, such as "irresponsible," "bullying," or "sloppy."
- Good feedback **is timely.** The closer the feedback is to the conduct discussed, the less opportunity for memory and rationalization to create disagreements on the facts of the behavior. Delay is appropriate if privacy is desirable, such as when providing feedback to a superior or when the individual is too emotionally distraught to be able to listen to the feedback.
- Good feedback **is usable.** The focus should be on how the individual can change her behavior in the future. If the moment for action has come and gone, with no opportunity for a future recurrence, feedback would not only be futile but also may create resentment.

The National Institute of Trial Advocacy (NITA) uses the following formula when its instructors provide feedback to participants who are learning deposition, trial, or negotiation skills; the stages can be adapted to cover many other situations when feedback is essential:

(1) **Headline:** identify the point you want to discuss, using a short introductory phrase;

(2) **Playback:** as close as possible to the event, describe the behavior or repeat the comment you want to critique;

(3) **Prescription**: suggest a different way of approaching the event or phrasing the language;

(4) **Rationale**: explain why you think the listener should try a different approach.

Like all good approaches to feedback, the NITA system focuses on description and analysis as opposed to characterizing and conclusions (e.g., "I liked that question." "That summary of the facts was misleading."). This system of description and analysis works best, however, when there is a power-differential, such as the instructor-student, supervisor-supervisee relationships, or when the speaker is clearly an expert and the listener has sought out that expertise to improve. If this system is used between peers, the defense mechanisms protecting a person's self-concept may lead some lawyers to argue with the speaker especially at the Playback or Rationale stages (e.g., "You didn't summarize my question accurately." "The rationale for your approach doesn't make sense, given what I was trying to achieve with this question."). While clarification is an important step in receiving and evaluating feedback, beware of inviting arguments stoked by this approach, which emphasizes the speaker's superior experience and knowledge.

Other standard advice for giving feedback is to start with the positive comments about someone's performance before addressing areas that can be improved. Others advise that you should provide twice as many positive comments for every negative comment. However, both of these observations do little to address the barrier of individual self-concept and the degree to which people will defend theirs. Take the common "good, but ..." structure of typical feedback: "That was a well-written memo, but it was twenty pages too long." The listener with a hyper-critical self-concept focuses only on what follows the "but." The listener with an overly healthy self-concept hears only what precedes it. There is a popular maxim that explains this: "*BUT*" might as well stand for "*B*ehold the *U*nderlying *T*ruth." When people hear it some listeners only listen for the "ax" to drop, while other listeners just ignore the ax entirely. To reduce the number of "buts" in your feedback, here are two strategies. First, try taking the "but" out of your sentence and replacing it with "and." (Scott, 2004). Listen to the difference: "That was a persuasive memo, and it was twenty pages too long. The next time you write, your challenge is to present with the same forcefulness in a shorter space." The positive reinforcement is clear, as is the direction for improvement. Second, replace the "but" with a question. "That was a persuasive memo. Do you think you could shorten it by twenty pages to improve it?" With these two strategies, there is no ax to drop or ignore. You have focused the listener on what needs to be done to improve the work.

Attorneys we spoke to discussed how to give feedback. "You can't just say, 'Who's in charge here?' or 'This is a mess!' Attorneys who did that did not last long." A senior associate, Wayne, illustrated the effectiveness of one of his supervising partners:

> The partner gives good feedback. He doesn't overwhelm you with too much at once. He sets a proper tone about what is negative so you can learn from it. For example, one time I forgot the estimate I gave to a client for the cost of some work. Instead of telling me that I made a big mistake, which I did, the partner said "I need to write down estimates I give to clients because I get burned all the time." He turned it into a comment about a mistake that he had made in the past.

Wayne contrasted this feedback with a situation in which he and his supervisor had been asked to work on an opinion letter for a client, an in-house lawyer. Wayne's supervisor and other lawyers involved acknowledged that the facts were bad for the client. Wayne had to work hard to find any argument in the client's favor. When Wayne and his supervisor met with the in-house lawyer to discuss the opinion letter, the lawyer said to Wayne, "I didn't like the opinion letter. Your analysis was weak." The in-house lawyer continued, "As in-house counsel, my view of outside counsel is that your relationship with us should be as if you are working for your brother's company. You should do everything for us the way you would for your brother's company." Wayne described his reaction, "I just nodded my head. But I'm thinking, 'You don't get that loyalty from me. You are going to get what I am required to give. I have a fiduciary duty to the client. That's what you'll get. I'll give more to someone I treat as a brother, but you are not worth going the extra mile for.'" He added that there was the potential to have a good relationship with this lawyer, but that the way the in-house lawyer treated him about the opinion, blaming Wayne for a weak analysis when the law was dead set against the client's facts, immediately made Wayne not want to do more. "I will work hard, and do a good job for a business relationship. But I will work extra hard for a personal relationship." For Wayne, the negative way in-house counsel delivered the feedback made the difference in framing a future relationship. When you give feedback, accept that you are not going to be able to change another person's personality or character. Then it becomes easier to focus on the important objective of identifying the behavior you want to see continue and the behaviors that you want to see change. If you are tempted to describe the quality you want a group member to change in more general or abstract terms (e.g., "I wish you would be a better listener."), start by breaking that generality down into observable parts ("I am not sure that you understand what I am saying.

Would you be willing to paraphrase what I've been saying so I can see if you understand my point?"). To help break abstractions down, ask yourself, "What would it look like if this person did what I want her to do?" Remember, you have a better shot at changing your group members' actions than changing their character traits.

Another technique for clearing the hurdle of your listener's self-concept is to try to avoid evaluative labels that "judge," "accuse," or "blame." Try to avoid using labels such as "good," "bad," or "ugly" when giving feedback, because they may get snagged on your listener's self-concept. Instead, focus on the desired *quantity* of actions, using words such as *more* and *less*, and on how the conduct influences you and your group. To do so, you can use phrases like, "I liked that you have started speaking up more in our meetings. I find your comments helpful in focusing our discussions"; "I wish you were on time to our meetings more often. I get frustrated when we spend time catching you up on what you missed"; or "I would like you to stop checking your e-mail or texts during our meetings. I feel ignored and unimportant." By keeping the focus on quantity of conduct as well as on the impact it has on you and others, you avoid pushing the self-concept hot-buttons of the person you are trying to influence. Moreover, feedback that focuses on conduct and its impact on others eliminates the danger of attributing motives or making negative assumptions about someone else's state of mind. Although we have come a long way in the science of brain scans, even the best of them do not allow us to interpret intent or motivation accurately.

When an attorney has to give feedback that she knows will disappoint her audience, she has to be even more careful. One of the government attorneys we spoke to noted that it helps for her to send her colleagues the bad information, like "noncompliance found," ahead of time. Then, when she talks to them, she uses a flat delivery. "I try to be neutral about it, not emotional. Then I use reflective listening to reflect back my colleagues' concerns. 'I hear what you are saying.' 'What can I do to support this?' 'What can I do to help?' I also empathize with colleagues. 'I understand that this feels overwhelming.' " Using this approach, this lawyer has been able to be far more effective collaborating with her non-attorney colleagues.

When time constraints permit, one of the most effective ways to provide feedback is to ask the individual to critique himself. The giver of feedback then becomes more of a moderator, asking questions to get the other persons to describe what is satisfactory, what needs improvement, and the plans for improvement. (Tugend, 2009). Becoming one's own best fair and reasonable critic would be ideal, but most people are either too hard or too easy on themselves to succeed without outside perspective and direction. The best course is to question the receiver to clarify her self-concept and goals; then you can provide specific suggestions focused on conduct instead of judgment or labels.

2.4.2 · Guidelines for Receiving Effective Feedback

It is much easier for most of us to give feedback than to accept it. The same powerful hurdle to giving effective feedback, a well-defended self-concept, is at work. In giving feedback, your goal is to overcome the listener's defenses to get the listener to change her performance. When receiving feedback, in contrast, your own self-concept is at stake. Moreover, the person giving you feedback may be inept, cruel, or oblivious to your fragile self-concept, pushing your emotional hot-buttons.

The good news, however, is that the only party to the feedback process that you have control over is yourself. You can be sensitive to the roadblocks you construct for yourself, you can control your reaction to others' feedback, and you can put that feedback to good use, improving your performance in the eyes of those on your team. There are essentially four parts to processing and using feedback effectively. The first step is **listening**, the kind of deep and thoughtful listening discussed in the previous section in this chapter. The second step is **clarifying** any ambiguous or vague feedback on your performance. Be careful to avoid *arguing* with the speaker. The goal here is to understand how the speaker interpreted what you did or what you said, not to correct the speaker's interpretation.

Once you think you accurately understand the speaker's comments, the steps become more difficult. If possible, take the third step and **delay reacting** to the feedback. If you are like most people, your initial response to feedback aimed at changing your behavior is to be defensive, especially if the criticized behavior is closely tied to your self-concept or fits your natural preferences. For example, a critique of your grammar or punctuation skills may conflict with your self-concept of being a proficient and skillful writer, and lead you to quickly reject the speaker's comments because "[the speaker] clearly does not know her stuff." Remember the earlier discussion of the MBTI. Just because you have certain preferences in thinking or communicating does not mean that you have more ability in those areas.

When receiving feedback, take time to weigh the comments of the speaker. Moreover, to cope with the barriers presented by your self-concept, play devil's advocate. Ask yourself to imagine the speaker is right. Can you then see how external perceptions of your performance might change? Is there a way those changes can be reconciled with your view of yourself in this context? For example, suppose you view yourself as a strong, take-charge, no-nonsense worker who gets the work done. The feedback you receive after a group project is that the other group members viewed your expression of your opinions and conclusions as domineering or stated too loudly and frequently. Instead of immediately refuting those observations (probably loudly and repeatedly!), first, try to view yourself from the outside, from the perspective of other group members. Would it be possible to state your views in a more quiet tone of voice but with the same degree of intensity, inviting the others to listen more willingly, so that you only need to make your point once? There is, after all, a modified self-image to adopt: that of the strong, silent type.

The final stage is **responding** to the feedback. If you want to affirm the feedback, you may want to tell the speaker something like the following: "Thank you for the comments you gave me on our draft appellate brief. I realize I just didn't see the number of errors in my Bluebook citations." Even better, go a step further and make the speaker feel that the effort to give feedback was meaningful by sharing your plan for changing your performance. For example, "John, I did not understand the level of anxiety I was causing you by sending you the draft of the Johnson contract so close to our final deadline. In the future, I plan to set an earlier, internal deadline for myself so we have adequate time to make changes based on the teams' suggestions."

In some instances you may feel that the feedback you received truly lacks merit, perhaps because the speaker is a poor listener. Her comments may be wholly inconsistent with other feedback you have received. The key skill is to demonstrate that you did hear, understand, and consider the feedback, even if you have decided not to adopt changes to the practices discussed. Assure the speaker that you understood what she was trying to say, even if you do not plan to change your behavior.

A major contributor to the success of any work group is the level of preparation and understanding you bring to the group. You have a lot of control over your ability to understand your own communication, thinking, and other preferences. When you understand that your preferred work modes are different from others', it is easier to accept that your preferences may not be the best modes of operating in all situations and to seek to understand others' strengths and contributions.

Similarly, you control your listening skills. Deep, meaningful listening requires constant attention and practice. You also have control over the tightly related skills of giving and receiving feedback. When giving feedback you may not control a listener's reactions, but you do have a high degree of control in anticipating and strategizing around your listener's defensive self-concept. And in receiving feedback, you have complete control over how you take in, react to, and use it. Finally, you have both control over and responsibility for your attitude and motivation for working collaboratively. As you are going to have to work with others, you can maximize your effectiveness by developing the skills that will enable you to work well with others.

Applications

1. Review the descriptions of the MBTI types in this chapter.

- Where do I find energy and strength: an external world of people, first-hand experience, and activity, or an internal world of ideas, theory, memory, and emotions?
- How do I perceive or absorb information?
- How do I organize and process that information?
- How do I come to conclusions or decisions?
- What type do you consider yourself? If possible, take the MBTI.

2. Thinking about earlier times in your life or other circumstances, compare your answers now with what they would have been then.

- Have you adapted to changes around you?
- If so, how comfortable are you with any changes?
- If not, does that limit what you can learn in your current studies and experiences?

3. Ask a colleague with whom you have recently collaborated for some informal feedback on your performance. Give the person advance notice and time to reflect. Consider putting a 15- to 20-minute, one-on-one meeting on their calendar. Ask specifically for candid feedback on what you did well, as well as what you need to improve. Take note of how the person delivers the feedback and be conscious of how you receive it in light of this chapter's discussion of self-concept.

Chapter 3

Group and Team Dynamics

3.1 · Introduction to Styles of Leadership

There is growing demand in the legal profession for better understanding of lawyers as leaders of nonprofit and for-profit institutions, leaders of teams within those institutions, and leaders of small work groups in diverse contexts. (Rhode & Packel, 2011; Rubenstein, 2008; Nischwitz, 2007; Heineman, 2006; Zwier, 2006). While leadership theories vary, everyone agrees one of the most important parts of a lawyer's career is to provide leadership—both as a member of the bar and as a citizen. The importance of leadership is illustrated in Ben W. Heineman, Jr.'s observations, in an essay he wrote while he was a Distinguished Senior Fellow at Harvard Law School's Program on the Legal Profession:

> Leadership can occur in strictly legal institutions—the bench, the bar, and law schools—or in social, political, and economic organizations. It can occur in the public sector or the private sector or the non-profit sector. It can occur in traditional institutions or in new institutions created by new leaders. It can lie in finding solutions for an existing agenda of issues or defining a whole new agenda. It can occur in policy or in politics. A person can lead as a specialist or as a generalist. He can lead in U.S. institutions or in global ones. She can lead as an insider, using power for good ends, but with inevitable compromises, as an outsider, seeking to speak truth to power without the responsibility of institutional authority. The leader can be a person of action or as a person of the mind whose ideas seek ultimately to affect action.

(Heineman 2006, p. 597).

Because leadership is an important contemporary topic, we briefly introduce some of the leading theories of leadership that most often apply to lawyers. It is helpful to understand these different leadership approaches so that you can recognize the leadership terminology, which is widely used in the business and nonprofit worlds. After this introduction, we will elaborate on one leadership approach—lateral leadership. We focus on lateral leadership because lawyers are frequently on the outside of an organization. Lawyers are clients' counselors, advisors, and problem-solvers. Lawyers may not be fully in charge of a situation, but how we approach collaborating with clients, their employees, or other constituencies is a form of leadership. Members of effective legal groups and teams have fundamental skills that allow them to lead without authority—to lead laterally. However, some of the other styles of leadership discussed below are more relevant when thinking of lawyers in their roles as leaders of their organizations, firms or practice groups, instead of in their roles as client representatives.

In the descriptions of the different types of leaders, consider the examples from your own experience in social and work settings. Each leadership style has positive and negative qualities; thinking about your own experiences may prompt you to recall good and bad examples of leadership you have experienced. In addition, remember that these styles may overlap or evolve for an individual leader, depending on the context and the person involved.

Three classic leadership styles are (1) authoritarian; (2) democratic; and (3) laissez-faire. (White & Lippett, 1960). We firmly believe that no one leadership style is better than others when it comes to being a successful legal professional; effective leadership depends on the situation, the kind of decisions that need to be made, and the people involved.

An **authoritarian leader** is "The Boss." Authoritarian leaders make decisions and give directions to their subordinates. Authoritarian leaders' subordinates are responsible for implementing their supervisors' decisions without question or contradiction. The authoritarian leader may not explain her rationale for a decision. She also may not reveal her overall goals and plans for the organization. The key is that power is centralized in the authoritarian leader.

The opposite of the authoritarian leader is the **democratic leader**. The democratic leader is a facilitator whose function is to assemble others to work together collaboratively. The democratic leader discusses all issues with the group, which works together to reach a result by consensus. The group sets the overall direction for the organization, not the leader. Here, the power rests completely in the group, of which the democratic leader is an equal member.

A **laissez-faire** leader claims the least power of all. The laissez-faire leader provides minimal direction to the group. Initiatives or changes in policy are initiated by the group. This kind of leader is responsive to requests for information and advice, but does not initiate it or volunteer it. This type of leader does not assign roles or direct work assignments.

In addition to these three classic styles of leadership, there has been much recent attention on three personality types of leaders: charismatic, transformational, and servant leaders. These studies blend descriptions of the leader's personal characteristics and traits with attention to the relationship between the leader and his followers. The **charismatic** leader attracts and inspires followers through a combination of personal charm, attractiveness, and unusually strong communication skills. Individuals who have been exposed to a charismatic leader commonly exclaim, "I felt as if I was the only person in the room." Researchers who have studied charismatic leaders note the ability of these individuals to read their social and emotional environments, sensing the emotions, moods, and needs of both individuals in the room and the group itself. Charismatic leaders use this information and adapt their verbal and nonverbal language to the situation and the people they are addressing. Examples of charismatic leaders range from some of the most despicable individuals in history to some of the most admired. This is partly because the charismatic traits can be described quite apart from the leader's moral development, self-awareness, intentions, and mental health.

The **servant leader** is defined by the leader's motivation and moral development. (Greenleaf, 2013; Spears, 1995). The servant leader seeks to meet the needs of individual members of the group while helping the group achieve its goals. The servant leader has strong listening skills and a sense of empathy—the ability to see the world from the perspective of others. This type of leader is supportive, even self-sacrificing, to help the organization improve. The servant leader can be the opposite of the charismatic leader, because the servant leader need not be in the spotlight or receive others' adulation or recognition. The servant leader focuses on the well-being of team members and the development of the team so all reach their full potential.

One of the most frequently discussed contemporary leadership types is the **transformational leader**. The transformational leader shares qualities of the charismatic leader and has the strong moral compass of the servant leader. The unique quality of a transformational leader is her capacity to create a compelling vision for the organization's potential future. She presents this vision as achievable if the organization's members work together. To create this powerful image, the transformational leader must have a deep understanding of the diverse needs, resources, hopes, values, and emotions of the organization, the willingness to challenge the traditional ways of thinking, and the ability to find the essential, but overlooked, threads that can be woven together to create the vision. The transformational leader needs an unusual degree of intelligence, interpersonal skills, and self-awareness.

To summarize, we will paraphrase and supplement Professors Steven A. Beebe and Timothy Mottet's comparison of how the different kinds of leaders might approach developing an organization's vision. An authoritarian leader would announce: "Here's your vision: now get it done." The democratic leader would ask, "What vision do we want?" The laissez-faire leader would not develop a vision unless specifically asked to do so. The charismatic leader would present a dazzling vision: "Here is what I can do!" The servant leader would ask, "How may I help you achieve the vision that would be best for you and your organization?" And the transformational leader would say, "Here is the vision that you and our organization have shown me we can achieve if we respect our values faithfully, use our resources wisely, and challenge but support each other always." (Beebe & Mottet, 2010).

While leadership is widely recognized as important to success in most fields, it is seldom treated as a skill to be learned and practiced. We agree that some people appear to have more natural leadership skills than others, but we firmly believe that lawyers can and should develop a range of leadership skills. As noted earlier, we emphasize that **lateral leadership**, or **leadership without authority** is an effective approach for many legal professionals, given the myriad tasks we are called upon to do for those we represent. This leadership style is consistent with the general theme of this book, which is that all members of effective legal groups or teams have leadership responsibilities, even if they are not in charge. Our overarching goal is to help legal professionals develop the underlying communication and conflict management skills that can make any type of leader more effective.

3.2 · A Practical Approach to Leadership for Lawyers

The roles and skill-sets of a lawyer who leads others are diverse and call for flexibility. One common thread for all effective leaders is the ability to collaborate well with others to accomplish individual and shared goals. Lawyers who are great leaders do not become so because of their solo work. They are leaders because of their ability to bring people together to accomplish shared goals, such as to structure deals, to change public policy, or to resolve private and public conflicts.

In this sense, leadership does not require official authority, being put in charge of others. This is because leadership of a group or team without authority does not mean you lack power. There are many types of power in small groups. (Beebe & Masterson, 2003). **Legitimate** power, which comes from being elected or selected to lead a group, is only one type of power. Power to lead also comes from **coercion,** the ability to punish or to create adverse consequences such as pay cuts or bad work assignments. For example, if you are on a law firm committee with someone with higher status in the firm, you are likely to treat that person as a leader even if no one is nominally in charge of the group. The positive counterpart of power based on coercion is power based on **reward,** the ability to give tangible perks or promotions to other members in the group. Taking leadership of a group based on the power to coerce or reward other members can create strong negative reactions from other members of the small group. There are two other grounds of power which successful legal professionals rely on heavily to lead when no one has been designated a leader with legitimate power. These are power based on being an **expert,** having special knowledge and information, and **referent** power, which comes from being well-liked and admired.

Roger Fisher and Alan Sharp identify the importance of **lateral leadership** in their book *Getting it Done: How to Lead When You're Not in Charge.* They use an extended example of a young law partner, who is frustrated with the lack of profitability at his firm. Like many confident, assertive legal professionals, the young partner's first response to this problem is to criticize the firm's managing partners publically at a partnership meeting, demanding that they alter their own perks and behavior before insisting on more work from the younger lawyers. Although the young lawyer is privately congratulated by his contemporaries for "speaking truth to power," the senior partners are unhappy with him—the only behavioral changes the managing partners make are directing more unpleasant tasks to the young partner. (Fisher & Sharp, 1999, pp. 62–63). Fisher and Sharp stress that the young partner must first develop the skill of leading himself, focusing on his individual purpose, before working on the organization's collective purpose. We agree, which is why Chapter Two of this book focuses on developing individual skills as a legal professional—doing the groundwork necessary to be a better leader—lateral or otherwise.

We will return to the concept of lateral leadership—and Fisher and Sharp's suggestions for the young law partner—elsewhere, but first we want to focus more on the link between leadership and working in small groups and teams. The common term for the crucial leadership skill of working well with others is **teamwork.** This phrase is probably second only to "leadership" in its current buzz value, but it is also misleading. Not all communication situations involving more than one person should be called teamwork. The quality and complexity of the communication among people who are assembled together can vary significantly. The interaction between two people—which communication theorists and social psychologists would call a **dyad**—differs substantially from the interactions among three or more people. Dyads face many of the same communication problems that small groups and teams face, so most of this book should be helpful even if you are one of two lawyers or law students working together. However, this book targets the more difficult scenarios—where three or more people come together to try to achieve at least one common goal—what we would call a **work group** or **team**.

Still, there are numerical limits to what we would call work groups or teams. A class of eighty-two Civil Procedure students constitutes a grouping or aggregation of hard-working individuals, but not necessarily a work group or team. Communication experts differ over the upper limit for a work group or team. Some would go as high as twenty-five members, but the more group members, the more likely there will be sub-groups, which complicate any one member's ability to analyze and influence group effectiveness. (Beebe & Masterson, 2003; Katzenbach & Smith, 1999). Work groups or teams generating legal work can range in size within these parameters, but a general rule of thumb for optimal working group size is five to seven members. (Cragan, Wright & Kasch, 2004). Of course, separate groups or teams can also come together to work toward a shared goal—cooperative alliances. Or there may be competition among multiple teams to establish the supremacy of one team's goal. However, if one of these entities is not working effectively, the impact of the problems can expand exponentially when that entity must interact with others. Conversely, a strong small group can help carry weaker ones toward the shared goal—or in a competitive arena, trounce its competition.

In addition to the numbers of participants, another quality of groups and teams is that they are composed of individuals who gather to achieve at least one common purpose that they cannot accomplish as well individually as they can with others—the participants are interdependent. (Lewin, 1951). Recognizing the interdependent quality of legal work groups and teams is critical to their success. For example, one of the common approaches to group work is to take a project or assignment, such as an appellate brief, break it up into subparts so that each group member researches and writes one part of the brief—and then merge the separate parts together before the deadline. This can result in a perfectly acceptable brief, but rarely results in a great brief. Moreover, some projects, such as complex corporate deals or complex litigation, are not easily subdivided. This divide and try to conquer shortcut to collaborative work is generally not as successful as facing up to the interdependent nature of group work and using the strengths of the group approach to produce a better result. We will say more about this shortly when we discuss the pros and cons of working collaboratively. But first we must make a crucial distinction that is lost in most of the popular business literature on teamwork, but will not be lost on legal professionals.

Because people gather for many different purposes, there are many different kinds of small groups and teams. See Figure 3.1 for the variety of common groups and teams one finds in the legal context.

Figure 3.1 · Examples of Types of Legal Groups or Teams and Key Characteristics

Examples of Legal Groups or Teams	Key Characteristics
Law School Work Groups Appellate Courts	• One-time or on-going meetings • Composed of peers • Focus is on sharing information, task-completion or decision-making
Governance Groups (Boards of Directors, Committees)	• Generally on-going meetings • May be composed of participants of different status • Can represent a diversity of backgrounds or skill sets • Policy or decision-making focus on a range of goals
Ad Hoc Groups (Task Force, Blue Ribbon Committee)	• Limited meetings • May have members of varied status and skill sets • Limited goals
Business Teams	• Ongoing meetings • Composed of members of varied status and skill sets • Organized by substantive area of law (e.g., The Intellectual Property Team) or Client/Case (The Ford Team, The Cambrio Prosecution Team)
Executive or Managerial Teams	• Ongoing meetings • Composed of high level peers • Decision, policy-making, and strategic planning focus

To summarize, a work group is composed of a small number of individuals who are interdependent, gathered together to accomplish at least one shared goal. But how does a work group differ from a team? Only some groups become—or are intended to become—teams. To play a bit of a logic game here, all work teams are task groups, but not all such groups are teams. See Figure 3.2.

Figure 3.2

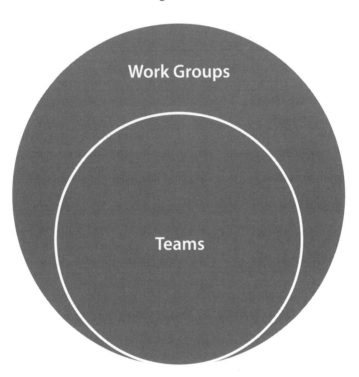

Both work groups and teams are important to law students, law schools, law firms, government agencies, corporate in-house counsel, legal service providers, legislative bodies, and all other legal entities. By drawing a distinction between work groups and teams, we do not mean to trivialize the importance of work groups. On the contrary—sometimes there is no need for a work team because a good group can be just as successful in accomplishing its goals. Indeed, because we believe that work groups are so pervasive and important in the legal environment, we seek to help legal professionals feel more comfortable working collaboratively and become more successful working as part of a team.

Nevertheless, the distinction between task groups and work teams is significant. A work team represents a higher level of commitment and function-

ing to the operation and goals of the group. Here are the essential characteristics that transform a work group into a team:

- Teams are intentionally composed of team members with a range of complementary skills and perspectives;
- Team members are individually committed to the success of the entire
  team in reaching shared goals;
- Team members strive to interconnect their contributions as the project
  develops, maintaining more frequent communication and developing a
  more cohesive approach;
- Team members hold each other accountable for achieving the team's goals;
- Team members develop a new self-image as part of "the team," which can
  have a unifying and motivating effect on both the members' and the collective group's performance.

(Johnson & Johnson, 2006; Lumsden, Lumsden & Wiethoff, 2010; Katzenbach & Smith, 1999). Some writers ignore the difference between work groups
and teams, but we think this conflates the basic definition of a work group or
team with the benchmarks of a successful work group or team.

You may not care about the labels "work group" or "team," but it is important to understand that work groups can be effective without having the higher-
level qualities of a team. More importantly, simply calling a group a "team"
will not make it one. We made a similar point in Chapter Two—there is a big
difference between working well cooperatively and working well collaboratively. To work well cooperatively, where there is a low level of interdependence and individual accountability, you do not need the level of thought,
planning, and care that goes into creating a real "team," where there is strong
interdependence and joint accountability.

Calling a group a team can also be counterproductive if the task is not appropriate for teamwork. This can happen when:

- the time pressure is too great to allow for collaboration;
- the individuals available to serve do not have the necessary range of skills
  to accomplish the objective;
- the goal or objective of the group is not clearly defined; or
- the group is so permeated with conflict that the necessary team characteristics of interdependence and commitment to joint accountability are
  missing.

Calling a group of legal professionals a team under these circumstances is just
likely to produce the kind of disillusionment that gives "teamwork" a bad name,
reinforcing some lawyers' cynicism toward collaborative work.

Understanding the difference between groups and teams is especially important when you are responsible for assigning work—for example, as a general counsel organizing the work of in-house counsel, a supervising prosecutor in a County District Attorney's Office, or a law professor using group work in class. Understanding the difference is also important when you are a member of a group—what is expected of you and your colleagues? If your supervisor has dumped you with some colleagues and called you a team, as a preliminary matter, spend some time figuring out whether everyone understands the level of commitment that a team involves. If they do not, ask the supervisor to clarify or modify the expectations—the supervisor's or those of the would-be members of the team.

3.3 · Moving from Good Group Member to Effective Team

We have already discussed the qualities necessary for you to participate competently in a legal work group:

- positive attitude toward group work;
- self-awareness—of your own preferences, strengths, and weaknesses;
- understand and appreciate the differences in others—whether based on personality preferences, personal characteristics, or culture;
- effective listening skills; and
- ability to give and receive effective feedback.

For most legal professionals, however, being competent is rarely sufficient. We constantly push ourselves to be better. Thus in this chapter we chart the characteristics of an effective team. Put another way, this chapter focuses on moving you from being a competent group member to becoming part of a great team.

Every management consultant has his own checklist of the ideal team, with some variations. But there is substantial agreement on the fundamental elements of effective teamwork. In addition to the qualities of a good group member, the members of a good team:

- commit to at least one clear shared goal;
- have strategically diverse skills, abilities, experience, and perspectives;
- recognize their role in the team and appreciate the roles of others;
- respect their interdependence; and
- accept joint accountability.

Although these elements obviously overlap (e.g., joint accountability creates interdependence), each element merits separate discussion.

3.3.1 · An Effective Team Has at Least One Shared SMART Goal

This may be the most crucial component of developing effective teams. A work group may be able to function to some degree with a vague sense of what its individual members would like to accomplish. This describes most routine committee work, for example. But a team's effectiveness depends on all team members committing to at least one clear common goal. Having a team goal—or set of goals—is essential because goals provide: (1) direction—a compass to guide team action; (2) motivation—goals energize the team, especially during hard times; (3) common ground for resolving conflict—goals provide the space where divided team members can come together; and (4) criteria for assessment and evaluation of team performance. (Johnson & Johnson, 2006).

Lawyers, with their pragmatic bents, frequently talk about the necessity of having concrete goals, as opposed to abstract goals. The most common formula for framing helpful goals is the acronym SMART. (Johnson & Johnson, 2006, p. 74; Doran, 1981). Although there is a surprising range of terms for the acronym, it is a helpful mnemonic in any of its formulations. We are providing our preferred terms below as our best advice for stating clear shared goals. To be valuable, a goal must meet every one of the SMART criteria. Thus, a SMART goal must be:

- **Specific.** The goal must be sufficiently defined so that the team can break it apart into its components—create an action plan, or series of steps, to achieve it. *Tip:* Stick to stating your goal in nouns and verbs—who, what, when and where. Keep the adverbs out (e.g., "quickly," "efficiently," "cost-effectively").
- **Measurable.** Team members should be able to track their progress on achieving the goal. This factor is essential to maintaining team motivation by providing targets. *Tip:* The goal should answer these questions: When will we know we hit the target? How will we know we hit the target?
- **Attainable.** At least in theory. This SMART criterion is somewhat ambiguous. To some, the "A" should be "Aspirational;" others say it should be "Ambitious." Still others are fine with "Acceptable." *Tip:* our advice is that the more "Ambitious" the goal, the higher the level of team "Ability" it requires—the goal ordinarily should be tailored to the capacity of the team. However, a "stretch" goal—one that challenges the team—can

be powerfully motivating, pushing a team beyond what it thought it could "Accomplish."

- **Relevant.** The goal must have intrinsic value to the team members. It must appeal to their individual interests, even though the goal is to be shared by all. Psychologists say that to motivate, a goal must have "salience"—it has to feel worthwhile and consistent with an individual's needs or desires. *Tip:* Each member of the team should be able to explain why the goal matters to her.

- **Time-Bound.** A goal usually needs an expiration date. Those of us with a Myers-Briggs "Perceiving" preference understand the need for providing a deadline—we are capable of endless searching and working to find better outcomes, unless something—like a goal—tells us to stop. Some writers find other uses for the "T," such as "Transfer"—the goal should let the members take what is learned and transfer it to new situations. (Johnson & Johnson, 2006, p. 74). This makes particular sense for stating educational goals.

Figure 3.3 provides contrasting examples of whether a goal meets the SMART criteria.

We are spending the bulk of our discussion on this element of team effectiveness because it is essential that a team have at least one clear shared goal. But who is responsible for setting team goals? Usually, the person or persons responsible for bringing the team together will likely make the initial attempt to explain why the team is being created, or there may be some obviousness to the existence of the team, such as when a law partner in the Mergers and Acquisitions Department brings in a new deal and puts together a deal team. But it is highly possible that the creator of the team will not sufficiently explain the purpose of the team with the kind of precision that creates SMART team goals. Moreover, the complexity of the team project may require long-term, mid-term, and short-term goal setting. The goals of a team drafting the initial complaint in a class action will be framed differently than those of a team entering preliminary settlement discussions, although they obviously interrelate. And to be fair, sometimes goals cannot be clearly stated until there has been some initial fact investigation or other preliminary work. No matter who sets the team in motion, an effective team is likely to spend considerable time stating, clarifying, and testing its goals under the SMART or similar framework.

Recall Fisher and Sharp's story of the young law partner, who was frustrated with his firm's lack of profitability. The partner's first tactic was to lash out publically at the managing partners. He quickly realized, after their negative response, that this was unproductive. After some reflection, he realized he had

Figure 3.3

Goal	Specific?	Measurable?	Attainable?	Relevant?	Time-Bound?
In the criminal law course, we will understand how a criminal trial works.	What does "understand" mean? What aspects of a criminal trial are you talking about?	In theory, but not in practice. We don't know what your "understanding" will look like, or how you will demonstrate it.	Unclear. Scholars have spent lifetimes seeking to understand crime and punishment.	Somewhat. It depends on the degree of "understanding." Some students want to practice transactional law, some just want to pass the class.	No deadline defined. Implied deadline is by the end of the semester.
By the end of class on Monday, we will create a visual aid to illustrate the stages of a criminal trial, from charging a defendant to sentencing.	We know what needs to be done and when. Could it be more specific? Probably, but one needs to find the balance between setting the goal and letting the team do the work. For example, the team needs to figure out what kind of visual aid it will chose, how it will define the phases of the trial, and which members will do what part of the work.	We know when it will be clear if the goal has been met—by the end of Monday's class, and what outcome we expect to see (a visual aid).	The goal is well within the ability of a team of first-year law students, but might be a stretch for a team of middle-school students.	Each member of the team can see how creating this visual aid will help him or her become more knowledgeable about the criminal trial process, a goal that fits with other meaningful individual goals, such as passing the course and passing the bar exam.	By the end of class on Monday.

not given them positive suggestions for improvement. The young partner came to the next partnership meeting with his own statement of the firm's goals, and moved to put them to a vote. He promptly discovered that the senior lawyers and managing partners did not appreciate being told what their goals should be; his motion lost by a landslide.

While acknowledging that there is no one right strategy for the young partner, Fisher and Sharp recommend a multi-step process in this common situation. First, *ask* for data—ask those in charge for their understanding of the loosely-defined goal you and your team are asked to accomplish. When asking for data, frame the question in terms of medium-term and short-term goals. So, for example, if the law firm's mission statement is "being known for the highest standards of excellence in the practice of law," the young partner might initiate a conversation about the goal with one senior colleague, "Chris, what do *you* think that means for the firm in the next five years?" Then, after listening actively and carefully, ask for an even shorter-range target that follows from the senior lawyer's initial reaction. Here is an example, loosely based on Fisher and Sharp's version to reflect more current reality.

> Chris, I understand your point about the slow recovery our clients are experiencing with their businesses. When I'm thinking two years down the line, I'm wondering what kind of business development goal we could commit to if we think about a combination of obtaining new clients and growing current clients—what would you think of 7 percent growth in client billings over the next two years?

(Fisher and Sharp, 1999, p. 66).

The job of this young lawyer is to lead laterally; it will not work to verbally beat up his colleagues or just tell them what to do. He needs to start one conversation that he will seek to share with other senior lawyers, *asking* for their answers to the same questions—"what would our business look like to you in five years? In two years?"

The next step is to *offer* information showing why the current goals do not work for you or your team. For example, a current goal appears incapable of being measured, and that hurts your ability to produce the best results for the team. Sometimes, however, a goal is deliberately vague because of lack of agreement about what the goal should be. In Fisher and Sharp's example, the young partner learns, through his conversations, that the lack of direction in the firm may come down to an internal disagreement about the proper level of support staffing. In that situation, they suggest that the lawyer *offer* his colleagues a diagnosis of the underlying disagreement, but not the treatment. The final component of this process is to "offer a do next"—offer to draft a set of mid-term and short-term goals for "preliminary comments and mark-up"—not for formal action of any kind. That produces more conversation toward resolving the disagreement that can be reshaped ultimately into a draft of a more formal proposal, but one which can be offered by those in charge. The point of the lateral leadership process is to nudge your colleagues, especially those with more power, into creating better goals—not by blaming them for their bad work or telling them what to do, but by coaching them toward SMART goals that will work for you and your team.

Fisher and Sharp brilliantly capture the frustration and urgency of the young partner, wanting to just tell his firm to get its act together. Lawyers are sometimes short on patience in planning, preferring to get right to work. Thus, a time-consuming process like lateral leadership seems excruciatingly painful. But skipping or short-circuiting the goal-setting process of teamwork is the most serious mistake a legal team can make. Time spent clarifying the team's shared goals and developing an action plan to achieve them saves time in the long run. Having one or more SMART goals team members avoid wasting time by doing pointless tasks that do not contribute to the ultimate goal.

Spending the time to clarify the team's purpose, goals, limits, and ultimate result is key. If the team members cannot agree on what to do, why to do it, and where they are headed, then their formation will not lead to meaningful results. As discussed more below, team diversity will lead to different views, but all teammates should be united in understanding their team's purpose, goals, limits, and the desired end. Team members can and should disagree and explore the research, data, options, and relative benefits and costs of the final product, but all should occur within the same, clear parameters.

For example, picture a group of young associates in a firm who are given a client problem that crosses a variety of areas. The supervising attorney tells the group to explore all possible issues. The supervising attorney fails to mention issues she sees or ask the group of associates to research potential remedies. The associates' resulting research might only focus on their areas of common knowledge and those closely related to them. In the end, the associates are limited by not knowing what they do not know, and by lacking the direction and insight of someone with more expertise. These novice lawyers are likely to ask clarifying questions, some of which may show their limited perspectives, but their limits may only fully surface after they have reached the assignment's deadline. This problem could have been avoided by the supervising attorney leading a discussion of the problem, with a follow-up meeting to discuss an initial sketch of the claims. Today's clients demand efficient and cost-effective legal services. Legal teams cannot afford to waste time because they were too impatient to be clear about their goals.

3.3.2 · An Effective Team Possesses Strategically Diverse Skills, Abilities, Experience, and Perspectives.

Effective teams include visible demographic diversity such as ethnicity, race, and age, and less visible personal diversity such as backgrounds, experiences, values, sexual preference, and personality types. (Sweet & Michaelsen, 2012; Johnson & Johnson, 2006). While diverse groups of people tend to have an initially lower level of group cohesion, after working together, diverse groups perform more effectively on complex tasks. (Johnson & Johnson, 2006, pp. 447–453). As this chapter's introduction notes, this component of effective teamwork works in conjunction with others. Effective communication, empathy, and understanding different roles help make diversity an asset on a team, even though it may present initial challenges. Whenever information and preferences can be expressed openly, a heterogeneous team will almost always reach better decisions because the resources within a heterogeneous team are much greater (Id.).

While the research supports the value of having diverse team members, this can present challenges. Many of us are usually most comfortable being around those who are like us, in attitudes, work styles, thinking approaches, and personalities. This is why it is important to understand your personality and preferences, whether through the Myers Briggs Type Indicator framework discussed in Chapter Two, or some other method. Those of us who enjoy thinking about the big picture and conceptual ideas can find talking about necessary details incredibly tedious. Those who find it easier to grasp a new concept by seeing concrete details and examples can become frustrated when a discussion focuses on abstract ideas. In working on a project, it is much easier to work with someone whose approach is similar, such as someone who most effectively processes material verbally collaborating with a colleague who similarly benefits from having to talk through the process.

For these reasons, as you become more aware of your preferences, it is tempting to gravitate toward others like yourself, but it is best to always try to seek out those with different preferences and skills. As with identifying complementary skills and aptitudes, you will be more effective in working with a diverse team if you expect to encounter diverse perspectives, views, and approaches, see them as learning experiences, and use these diverse perspectives to collectively improve the team's performance.

In addition to diversity of characteristics and preferences, teams need to have sufficient intellectual and social emotional talent and skills to accomplish complex tasks. To achieve high-level performance, teams need to include complementary skills and aptitudes, as individual members all have strengths and weaknesses. No sports or production team should have the same talents; teams thrive when the members of the team have complementary and compatible skills and aptitudes. Having teams include compatible and complementary skills and aptitudes works with the previous component of having each individual understand her role in the team. Effective teams include complementary skills, and recognize and work with each other's strengths and weaknesses.

For example, a team of public interest lawyers had complementary approaches to addressing their very low-income clients' housing problems. One attorney sought to create positive interpersonal connections with the public housing director, seeking to establish regular and open channels of communication. In this way, she sought to prevent clients from being evicted by having regular conversations with her clients and with the public housing officials about problems as they arose. Her goal was to identify problems early on, intervene to see if a solution could be reached, and help negotiate an acceptable plan with the client and public housing officials before the client received an eviction notice. Her experience was that by the time the public housing director issued an eviction notice, problems had escalated to the point where it was extremely difficult to negotiate.

In contrast, another lawyer on the team took a more litigation-based approach to protecting the clients' housing interests. When a client received a notice of eviction, or complained about a problem with public housing, this attorney sought to identify as many legal issues as possible, and then file a complaint against the housing authority. Other attorneys and paralegals on the team had complementary skills of working with social service agencies to help clients find alternate housing, locate sources of public assistance, and obtain job development training. All of these approaches collectively benefited the clients more than one approach would alone. While communicating regularly and openly with the public housing director helped solve many problems, when clients faced eviction and the multiple problems associated with it, litigating and gathering additional resources were critical.

The value of teams having complementary skills and aptitudes is easily seen in law school competitions. For example, in national moot court competitions, student teams perform best when they have complementary skills in areas such as developing a theme, analysis, research, organization, writing, citation, time management, attention to detail, verbal fluency, answering questions orally, quick thinking, oral persuasion, memorizing, and projecting confidence. "[I]f a team were to consist of brilliant speakers who are not able to write a scholarly memorandum, the team would not work well." (Moens, 2007, p. 630).

3.3.3 · An Effective Team Recognizes and Appreciates the Different Roles of Its Members.

This may be one of the more challenging aspects of teamwork and teams in general. Teams vary in their level of equality among teammates, and it is imperative to understand these different levels when they exist. For example, a group of law school classmates working together in a team during a course is an example of an egalitarian team. No one has more authority than others, none of the students is formally designated to be the leader, and no one student has greater influence over the team's decisions. As described below, in this situation, all team members share leadership.

Contrast this with a group of attorneys and staff working together in a legal organization. Assume in this latter situation, the team consists of five attorneys, a part-time law student clerk, and a paralegal. The five attorneys, including the supervising attorney, each have a different level of experience. The team is under the leadership of the supervising attorney, who has more authority than others over the team's decisions, can allocate tasks within the team, and is ultimately responsible for the team's performance. Among the others on the team, some may have more experience and traditional superiority, but others may have more specialized expertise, shaping the direction and responsibilities of the team. Nonetheless, Fisher and Sharp's example of a young law partner working to increase firm profitability demonstrates that even when you are not in charge, you can take a lateral leadership role. Understanding your role or roles in a team is crucial to helping your team become cohesive and working effectively.

As with the example of law students working on a team as a group of equals, when you are on an egalitarian team you will have no defined or recognized leader who will distribute responsibilities to the other members or exercise ultimate control. In law school there well may be someone on the team who thinks of herself as the team leader, but other team members may not recognize any authority and may resent her trying to assert authority over others. When teams lack a defined leader, the team members themselves need to decide how their team will function. They may decide to use a consensus decision-making model, discussed in the next chapter. In that model, a group can only come to a decision if all the group members agree on the proposed plan. To attain the most productive role for the team, each team member must be realistic about her skills. (Reilly, 2000, p. 596). For example, assume a team of law students is assigned to prepare the most effective license agreement. Mutiara is skilled at using precise language, Omar is excellent at thinking through all the analytical steps, Yoon has extensive licensing experience, Amanda excels at project management, Ryan enjoys examining all the possible problems, and Frances explores creative alternatives to conventional licenses. When this team decides how to approach designing their license agreement, they will ideally take into account their strengths and weaknesses to create the most efficient process and product.

Compare this model with a team which has a clear leader and other followers. Take the example of a managing attorney and his or her management team. In this team, there is a clear leader—the managing attorney—and followers—the management team. The only way a team like this works effectively is if each member understands her role. For example, the managing attorney must have positive interactions with other members of the team and show strong leadership qualities. For example, as described at the beginning of this chapter, a charismatic leader, one who leads others through personal charm and excellent communication skills, may show persistence and enthusiasm in pursuing long-term goals. (Waldman & Yammarino, 1999). Additionally, the role of the managing attorney is to help facilitate the best discourse among the management team. In return, the role of individuals within the management team is to support and facilitate ideas among each other. The management team must play off the managing attorney and vice versa. In doing so, a robust and impressive interaction among the individuals can occur that will resolve major concerns and accomplish important tasks.

Depending on a group's assigned tasks, size, and duration, some benefit comes from having designated roles. At times roles will naturally emerge, though in most instances some determination of roles is important to group functioning. Beyond a leader or shared leader, there are transactional or team-building roles (attending to relationship issues within the group—encouraging participation, managing conflict, helping team members connect and appreciate each other). Then there are task roles: identifying the team's procedure, organizing the meetings and discussions, providing critical thinking, ensuring that information is shared, and re-orienting the team to the task when the team is distracted. Depending on the task, several people may take on each role or the roles could rotate through team members.

Finally, if the team was created by or reports to someone outside the team, then that person's role must be clearly and carefully defined. If the outsider is not a member of the team or is a high, authoritative figure, then she must be cognizant of the deep impact she will have each time she interacts with the team. At times the outside authority figure may need to intervene in the team process, such as when the group lacks important direction, but gratuitous intervention could easily derail the team in quite unintentional ways. This type of intervention must be measured precisely.

3.3.4 · An Effective Team Respects the Team Members' Interdependence.

The strength and the weakness of a team is its interdependence. Creating and nurturing team interdependence requires a high degree of communication, empathy, and trust. While frequent communication is self-explanatory and easily taken for granted, it is important for all team members to recognize how important this is to having a group become an effective team. (Lencioni, 2002; Goleman et al., 2002; Forrester & Drexler, 1999; de Vries & Manfred, 2005).

As we discussed above, working on a team requires working with people who may not think, look, or act like you because of the need for diversity of characteristics, skills, and abilities. Empathizing with other individuals on a team gives you a greater understanding of their different perspectives and helps the team work effectively. Showing empathy helps communication, improves colleagues' moods, and resolves conflict. (Goleman, 2002). Empathy is not usually stressed in professional work environments or in the study of law, and is sometimes denigrated, as when President Obama cited then-Judge Sonja Sotomayor's capacity for empathy as one of her strengths when he nominated her for the United States Supreme Court. Leadership and communication experts, however, increasingly recognize the importance of empathy. People who show empathy excel "at recognizing and meeting the needs of clients, customers, or subordinates. They seem approachable, wanting to hear what people have to say. They listen carefully, picking up on what people are truly concerned about, and they respond on the mark." (Goleman, 2002, p. 50). Given this description, and the importance of reaching small group decisions on the U.S. Supreme Court, one would think that being empathic would be an asset for a member of this recently highly divided court.

As emotional intelligence expert Daniel Goleman notes, empathy "doesn't mean a kind of 'I'm okay, you're okay' mushiness." (Goleman, 2002, p. 50). Rather, as Goleman explains, empathy means trying to understand others' emotions, experience, and perspective, and responding appropriately to them. Recognizing others' feelings and perspectives can be a challenge for some of us. Others are more adept at putting themselves in the shoes of another, trying to see events from their perspective.

All of us, however, can develop our ability to empathize. To develop empathy, you must actively listen to your teammates as we described in Chapter Two. Observe them carefully, and seek to truly understand what they are feeling. Rather than jumping to conclusions, check your understanding with your teammates to determine whether your assumptions about what they are feeling are accurate. Does developing and showing empathy take energy? Yes, for most of us. Bear in mind that the skills you develop in doing so, as with the other components of effective teamwork, will help you on the job. Particularly as law practice becomes increasingly diverse and more of us interact with colleagues on a global level, being empathetic will help you navigate cross-cultural differences.

One attorney, Cora, described the importance of understanding her employees' backgrounds so that she could effectively empathize with them and help them be effective members of her team. One of her employees, Beth, had been working for Cora since she was 19 years old. Beth is now a single mother who works full time for Cora and is in her last year of law school. "Beth's been with me since the beginning, and I understand her circumstances and give her flexibility." While empathizing with her employee, however, Cora still maintains high performance expectations. "I also have to train Beth to communicate and respect her new manager. Beth needs to realize that she has to respect others' expectations, for example, that she needs to text or email if she is going to be late, even though she didn't need to do that for me because I understand the challenges she faces."

Finally, the interdependence of teams requires that its members trust each other. When trust is felt among team members, the team grows stronger and members feel that they can depend on one another. (Forrester & Drexler, 1999, p. 39). When team members fail to meet others' expectations, such as not completing an agreed-upon task during the time expected, trust is diminished, if not destroyed.

Trust is a complex concept—built through an interactive process of risk and validation, and destroyed through risk and betrayal. Trust turns on vulnerability. Team interdependence means team members are vulnerable and must depend on one another. When a team member's dependence and vulnerability is rewarded by beneficial treatment by other members of the team, trust increases. When a team member takes risks by opening up and sharing information, trust is destroyed when another abuses or exploits a team member. The creation and destruction of trust depends heavily on the psychological concept of reciprocity. (Cialdini, 2006). Reciprocity means team members will generally respond in kind to behavior they experience. The more open and supportive team members are to each other, the more they will experience the same behavior from others. Conversely, if a team member consistently withholds information, not reciprocating even when others self-disclose or otherwise show vulnerability, that team member is not as likely to be trusted. (Johnson & Johnson, 2006).

3.3.5 · An Effective Team Accepts Joint Accountability.

When teams are accountable for their collective performance, such as completing a project on the job, or producing an assignment in a course, the organization or professor signals that effective teamwork matters. Some advocates of using teams in educational settings stress that team projects should be a significant part of a course grade, reasoning that:

> [g]roups need an incentive for becoming an effective team and they need feedback on how well they are performing as a team. Graded group work meets both these needs. If a major part of the course grade depends on high-quality team performance, the individual and the team have the necessary incentive to work hard and to do well. In addition, the feedback on team performance, both graded and ungraded, gives teams the information they need to monitor and improve their performance as a team.

(Fink, 2004, p. 16).

Similarly, in a work environment, "accountability is the organization's way of saying that it makes a difference whether goals are reached or not." (Forrester & Drexler, 1999, p. 40). If, for example, a group of less experienced lawyers from the state department of insurance were teamed with physicians, health care workers, and patient advocates to design an effective health care incentive program, the insurance department lawyers would be more inclined to work together effectively to accomplish that goal if they knew that their department's directors would appreciate and reward them for collaboratively designing an effective program.

3.4 · The Qualities of "Super-Teams"

The previous sections focus on creating competent work groups and effective teams. Yet lawyers often want to be more than that; they want to be part of a team that consistently exceeds all expectations. Super-teams are teams that "weave together a rich fabric of competencies, experience, attitudes and values which create tightly woven, integrated cloth suitable for many purposes." (Hastings, Bixby & Chaudhry-Lawton, 1987, 10–12).

One can describe them according to their transactional, task, and systems processes. (Lumsden, Lumsden, & Wiethoff, 2010).

In their transactional processes, super teams have:

- **High expectations**—they have high expectations of themselves and each other and are constantly looking to improve their performance.
- **Flexibility with consistency**—they work best under principles and guidelines rather than strict rules, and maintain consistency through extensive communication.
- **Appreciation for their leaders and each other**—they value supportive leaders who generate direction and commitment; super-teams prize knowledge, competence, and hard work over the status of other team members.

In task processes, super-teams are:

- **Goal-driven**—they consistently reexamine, reaffirm or restate their goals, connecting them to the larger system's strategic plan and objectives, creating priorities and confronting obstacles to their objectives.
- **Creative and innovative**—they are flexible, taking risks to explore untried options and obtain potentially bigger gains.

In their relationships within systems, super-teams are:

- **Visible and accessible**—they build extensive formal and informal networks for assistance, communicating what they do and what they can offer other teams, which helps them when they seek reciprocal help.
- **Powerful**—they have responsibility, authority, and credibility within an organization because of their experience and performance.

To summarize, super-teams represent all the characteristics of a good group member and effective team, taken to the highest level of competence. These ideal teams may exist only temporarily, but they illustrate that the whole is greater than the sum of the parts.

3.5 · The Stages of Legal Teams

In addition to understanding the different characteristics of effective work groups, teams, and super-teams, it can be helpful to understand the different working stages that teams experience. Once you know these, you can more easily recognize the problems or issues that tend to arise in a particular stage. You can also help facilitate a smoother transition from one stage to the next when you know the group's current stage. Researchers have different names for these stages; we find the terms used in management theory most relevant to legal practice. Four working stages to identify are: **forming, storming, norming,** and **performing**. (Tuckman, & Jensen, 1977).

The **forming** stage is an orientation period in which the members of a group get to know each other, sharing basic information about themselves, and engaging in small talk. This stage is marked by superficial social interaction and tentative, cautious approaches to the group's tasks as the group starts to build familiarity, trust, and cohesiveness. Group members begin to develop opinions about their function in the group and the group's task. There is a high risk of false consensus in this stage; group members tend to be very deferential to fit in or keep the peace, not because they agree with each other. This stage is not a good time to try to decide complex issues, where critical thinking and argument will produce stronger work product. The group needs to develop a stronger foundation before that hard work can be done.

As group members develop more familiarity with each other, they may start to compete with each other for power. As they become more familiar with their task, they begin to assert their opinions more openly, leading to the next stage, **storming**. Some researchers also call this the conflict stage. While both terms have negative connotations, as we discuss elsewhere, constructive conflict can be very important to effective outcomes. In the storming stage, group members start to have deeper, more substantive discussion as group members take different directions on their task. On the relationship level, group members start to disagree with each other, as they analyze and question each other's data, research and opinions. The confrontation function is essential to effective group work. Group members who have been silent need to be encouraged to speak up so the group can hear other alternatives. If group members are afraid of conflict, they may not be willing to offer missing information or options, and in the end the entire group's work product will suffer.

As a group airs, explores, and tests ideas, potential solutions or decisions start to solidify. Some group members, who may have been opposed to specific positions or opinions, may start to open up to changing their minds. This stage is called **norming**. Here is one way to think of it:

> Think of a time when a group adopted a course of action that you had at first opposed. Did you support the group decision in the end? If so, you had to change your attitude along the way. How did that take place? Can you identify a time when you suddenly turned against your former position? Probably not. The change most likely was gradual. If you argue strongly for a position in [Stage 2—storming], it is hard to let go of that position all at once. Your ego simply will not stand for it. At the same time, you may feel a need to pull the group back together.

(Beebe & Masterson, 2000, p. 207). At this stage, members begin to sense internal and external pressure to settle disagreements within the group and finish their task. Group members start to soften their positions, making tentative or ambiguous statements, hedging or qualifying their earlier opposition to signal movement toward consensus. In a law student group writing a moot court brief, an example might be: "I still think we should research the due process issue in this case further, but I understand the need to finish this draft of the brief. Maybe we can revisit the issue after we see how we are doing on our page limits at the end of this round of drafting." These kinds of statements allow for rebuilding group coherence while reaffirming the value of testing and challenging the group's proposals. Thus, in this stage, we see the group returning to its norm or emerging from the necessary divergence and disagreements of the storming stage.

The final stage is **performing**, which is marked by a sense of good-will and accomplishment. If a group has tentatively worked through the forming stage, struggled to keep conflict constructive during the storming stage, and managed to re-integrate during the norming stage, at the performing stage a group can experience a sense of direction, consensus, and group identity. The communication at this stage tends to be highly reinforcing, with group members sharing credit for the outcome. For example, consider this conversation in a litigation team:

> "John, I know I questioned your judgment at times on this motion to exclude the other side's expert, but we got the client an amazing result; we could not have done it without your experience and guidance."
>
> "Well, I don't know about that, Linda, but if we didn't have your persistence and up-to-the-second knowledge of the case law in this jurisdiction, we would have definitely lost this motion."

This kind of reinforcing communication can strengthen relationships within a team, and thus the team itself, so that it can withstand even stronger conflicts on future tasks.

This model of group dynamics requires a few caveats. It not necessary for a group to experience every stage described here nor is it essential to experience the stages in a set order. In fact, a group may experience some or all of these stages on different issues within a particular task. The key is that when you recognize that your group is in a particular stage or moving to a new stage, you are in a better position to recognize and manage the issues that will come up. If focusing on the development stages of a team does not seem helpful, consider a simpler framework. Group communication operates on a task level and relational level. Task activities are those directly relevant to accomplishing the group's goal. Task activities include defining the problem the group is addressing, collecting and analyzing the data collected about the problem, and developing criteria for a solution or decision. **Relational activities** are those behaviors and communications that build or damage relationships among group members, such as criticism, praise, encouragement, trust-building, or destructive conflict.

Some researchers suggest that there is a third, deeper level of group dynamics—a **topical focus**. A topical focus reveals themes or deeper values that a group may have, but which are not task or relationship specific. For example, a law firm committee may be charged with the task of recommending changes in the firm's compensation system for partners and associates. The committee will engage in vigorous task activities, such as comparing their current system to the systems used at other law firms. The committee also may engage in relational activities, such as having dinner together before their meetings, or spending part of the meetings catching up with the highlights of members' lives outside the office. But all of these activities may be conducted against a background of a particular topical focus—the firm's tradition of supporting extensive pro bono work, which makes the firm less profitable than others its size. This topical focus, which is revealed by communications among group members where it surfaces, may serve as the real agenda for the group. (Bormann, 1975; Poole, 1983). The bottom line is that groups may find themselves at different points of development on task or relational activities, depending on the topics at issue; groups do not always develop with as a unified "package" on the task and relational levels.

Understanding group development and dynamics is important as it provides you with some analytical distance when problems arise. You can step back and think about where the problem is occurring or repeating, at which stage, or which type of group function is at issue: task or relational? At that point, you have a better foundation to strategize about different approaches. A group in the early stages of formation may just need more time to allow the members to get to know each other before the group can address the task in a meaningful way. For example, an eager member of a non-profit law team may need to slow down a bit when she suggests dividing up work for a large client matter five minutes after receiving the assignment. If her group tentatively agrees with her, it is most likely due to social concerns, such as a desire to please or fit in with other members, not because the group members think this is a good time for dealing with the project.

Or you may develop insight into a group by looking at it from the task-relational-topic focus framework. For example, a team of lawyers who are responsible for gathering considerable information about a business venture may be operating well on the relational level. On the task level they may also be may be making all the right legal judgments by asking all the right questions to define what they need to learn. The lawyers on the team may keep running into disagreement over the best approach to gathering and organizing the information because they have strong conflicting views about the business's values.

Applications

1. List examples of leaders who illustrate the different styles of leadership described in this chapter. These may be people with whom you have previously worked, public figures, or characters from fiction.
2. What kind of leader would you most like to be? Identify why you would prefer this leadership approach and explain its potential problems drawbacks.
3. Review the descriptions of the types of work groups and teams listed in Figure 3.1. Write down examples of each category of work group or team of which you have been a part, or which you have observed. Reflect on how the descriptions in Figure 3.1 match your experiences.
4. In a small group, take turns describing the highest-performing teams each of you has been a part of. Review the work group and team dynamics described in this chapter, and help each other identify them at play in one another's experiences. Next, try to identify other dynamics, even beyond those described in this chapter, which made your teams successful.

Chapter 4

Conflict Management in Legal Teams

4.1 · Understanding Conflict

In theory, all lawyers ought to be experts in coping with conflict. Many lawyers trained in the adversarial model of civil dispute resolution welcome a good fight. Contrary to this stereotype, however, many law students and lawyers cringe at the thought of conflict, especially with co-workers or members of their own team. Here is an example of a young associate's nightmare:

> When Barbara first arrived at the firm, she was assigned an experienced, very intelligent paralegal who had been with the firm for about ten years. "I knew that I knew nothing and she knew a lot more than I did. I thought I made it clear that I wanted to learn from her. But she was really snippy with me. I would prepare something, and she would throw it down on my desk and say, 'That's not the way to do it. You can't do it this way.' I would try to explain that I wanted us to work as colleagues." When things didn't improve, Barbara talked to one of the partners. "He told me, 'You need to control her, she's your paralegal.'" This was not helpful, as Barbara felt that she was trying everything she could and nothing was working. "I just started doing everything myself. This wasn't efficient, but I found working with [the paralegal] exhausting and not worth it. The situation was made worse because partners at the firm knew that the paralegal and I weren't working well together, and one of the partners was on the side of the paralegal."

Barbara's situation is common. Lawyers and law students may be ready to face conflict from individuals on the other side of a case, transaction, or competition, but are far less comfortable dealing with conflict on their own teams.

Consequently, as we learn to work well collaboratively, we need to face up to the possibility of conflict. Collaborative work almost always raises some conflicts among the participants. The goal is not to eliminate all conflict; conflict can be useful, leading to higher quality work product. Rather than trying to avoid or eliminate all conflict, we need to recognize the benefits of conflict, and anticipate and plan for working through different kinds of conflict. Just because conflict is almost inevitable in collaborative work does not mean that it is inherently unpleasant. However, group members' fear of conflict, or anxiety about having to address conflict, can be an unnecessary barrier to effective collaborative work. The best way to manage concerns about conflict is to:

(1)   understand the dynamics of conflict;
(2)   learn how to navigate conflict;
(3)   use conflict to improve the team work product; and
(4)   learn how to cope with extreme and destructive conflict.

The first step is to understand conflict's dimensions. Most people think of conflict as a specific disagreement, a quarrel, or a clash between people. The classic definition of conflict is "the interaction of interdependent people who perceive incompatibility and the possibility of interference from others as a result of this incompatibility." (Folger, Poole, & Stutman, 2009, p. 4). This definition reveals important features of conflict. First, conflict is an **interaction**; it is a process, not one particular event. A conflict may surface at a particular moment, but it began and evolved as a dynamic process long before the eruption became visible. For example, Barbara's conflict with the paralegal started as soon as her assignment did, but the conflict took on a life of its own leading to the point where it was visible to other lawyers at the firm.

Second, conflicts arise when people are **interdependent**. If we do not have to think about ongoing connections with others in our group, we can simply walk away from each other with few consequences. Conflicts emerge when we care about our professional, personal, or social relationships with others, or when we must otherwise depend on others. For example, as an associate in a law firm, Barbara could not do her work by herself. Organizing discovery, investigating facts, and preparing documents required Barbara to work with other professionals in the firm. And the paralegal, as intelligent and experienced as she was, could not practice law; she needed Barbara's supervision and authority to do her job responsibly. As discussed earlier in Chapter One, when people work collaboratively, they have some degree of interdependence. Because they are interdependent, they have the potential for conflict.

Serious conflict arises when interdependent individuals have incompatible goals. However, one of the most common types of conflict in legal contexts arises when interdependent individuals perceive that they have incompatible strategies to accomplish their shared goals. For example, a team of lawyers may understand that their client wants a business transaction completed, and each lawyer depends on the others to reach that goal, but the lawyers have very strong opinions about the best strategies to accomplish the client's goal. Each firmly believes that his or her approach is the most effective and should be adopted by the team.

Regardless of the nature of the perceived incompatibility, the crucial quality of conflict is that it is interactive. Conflict involves exchanges among individuals and groups. Conflict can be interpersonal, such as conflict between individual group members. Conflict can also occur between groups. People in groups interact through a wide range of verbal and nonverbal communicative behaviors. As Professors Putnam and Folger explain, "fundamental to all conflicts are the series of actions and reactions, moves and countermoves, planning of communication strategies, perceptions, and interpretations of messages that directly affect substantive outcomes." (1988, p. 350).

As in all communication situations, these interactions can be complex, especially if the conflict is between more than two individuals. There is no silver bullet to resolve all types of conflicts. However, the good news is that because conflict is inherently interactive, no single person can completely control a conflict. Each person involved in a conflict has some degree of control over how the conflict unfolds. Just realizing that you are never powerless within a conflict can help you manage any apprehension about conflict.

Another key aspect to understanding conflict is that it operates on different levels. Researchers have different labels with different nuances for these dimensions of conflict. To simplify the nuances of conflict we suggest that all conflicts operate on a **relationship level** and at a **task level**. The relationship level generally involves problems such as perceived lack of trust, honesty, respect, and empathy. Conflict at the task level tends to be particular to each work situation, although there are some tasks that are generic tasks for small groups, such as picking a meeting place, setting an agenda, recording group transactions. Cora, who has been in practice for only seven years, is a real estate lawyer who runs her own firm and is very aware of these different types of conflicts. Cora has five attorneys and several paralegals working for her in two separate offices, one in a smaller city, one in a larger. Cora has noticed a real distinction in the qualities of relationships in the two areas. In the smaller city, people on opposite sides enjoy each other, have civil, cordial, and healthy relationships. In contrast, Cora notes that in the larger city, making real estate deals is much more adversarial. "People put the 'v' in seller v. buyer." She responds by trying to help the parties focus on resolving the business issues. Cora has learned to stop everyone when conflicts escalate, saying, "Let's take a step back. We all have the same goal, to close the transaction. Let's only focus on those things that will help us move forward to closing the transaction."

Cora applies the same principle—separating the task conflict from the relational conflict, in managing her staff.

> My policy is to never get upset or angry. I focus on solving the problem and not letting it happen again. For example, recently someone in my office failed to accurately calculate per diem interest, which meant that there was going to be a shortfall in payments as calculated. It's not productive to blow up, throw a fit. My strategy in the office is to fix the problem. I never engage my employees at the time. Later—up to a week later—I will sit down with them. I will address the underlying issue—"How can we make this a helpful experience? How can we prevent it in the future?"

The relational and task dimensions of conflict can be deeply intertwined, but when diagnosing and managing a conflict it helps to focus on them separately. Moreover, recognizing the different dimensions reveals the positive quality of conflict. On the task level, conflict can lead to a significantly better end product. For example, conflict that focuses on challenging and clarifying data, information, ideas, suggestions, and proposals can produce more effective solutions to problems. We discuss this useful dimension of task conflict in Chapter Five, when we discuss decision making in groups. The problem, however, is that if the relationship level of conflict is ignored or damaged in the process of working through the task, group members are less likely to produce good work product. This is because some group members may try to withdraw from the conflict, withholding information or ideas. Groups work more effectively than individuals only if the group uses the resources provided by each member. Moreover, if group members address the conflict on a task level, but dismiss or ignore the relationship conflicts, they are likely to generate fragile solutions that can be easily undone. Finally, because past damage to relationships haunts subsequent interactions, conflicts in relationships will persist and diminish the group's potential to work together effectively in the future.

To summarize, the key is not to try to eliminate all conflict. Instead, people working collaboratively need to understand why conflict arises, how conflict can be used to make the team more successful, and what to do when conflict becomes excessive or destructive conflict.

4.2 · Sources of Conflict

Research in conflict management, which is also called conflict resolution, has produced a wide range of concepts, theories, explanations, and terminology as thoughtful people try to develop better ways of understanding and coping with conflict. In doing so, researchers have identified many sources, kinds, and styles of conflict. This chapter summarizes the material we think is most helpful to legal professionals as they work in groups. For a more in-depth study of conflict management, we recommend that you investigate the sources in the references.

The primary cause of conflict in groups is also the source of a group's strength: **difference**. Differences in goals, strategies, information, resources, needs, beliefs, attitudes, values, ethics, motives, personality types, abilities, power, control, expectations, culture, and interests can create conflict. (Schutz & Bloch, 2006). This list of differences as a source of conflict surprisingly lacks differences in communication. We know that communication is tightly linked to conflict, but it is not a causal relationship. Communication, either poor quality communication or a lack of communication, can make an existing conflict worse, but it is not generally a cause of conflict by itself.

The classic definition of conflict—"the interaction of interdependent people who perceive incompatibility and the possibility of interference from others as a result of this incompatibility"—suggests another main cause of conflict, **perception**. People in conflict "*perceive* incompatibility and the possibility of interference." As many of us have learned the hard way, colleagues rarely want to intentionally interfere with our attempts to achieve our goals. That is, our perceptions are often wrong.

Occasionally our misperceptions are pretty basic and even funny. We simply do not hear each other correctly. A few years ago, one of this book's authors, who played goalie for a "senior" women's ice hockey team, suffered through a tough game. In the locker room, she whined at the coach, asking, "What the heck just happened out there on the ice?" The coach replied, "You!" At least that is what Scallen heard. Thinking that her coach was blaming her for the loss, Scallen stormed out of the locker room, terribly upset. One of her teammates asked the coach what he said to make Scallen so mad. He was baffled, "I don't know—she asked me why we lost out there, and I said that it was just 'youth.' Those other gals were just a lot younger!" That conflict was quickly resolved.

More commonly, however, we hear accurately but misinterpret what we heard. Here, cognitive science research has been helpful in documenting two common cognitive errors: fundamental attribution error and self-serving bias. These cognitive errors are both consequences of our using **attribution processes** in interpreting our perceptions. Attribution processes rest on the principles notions that (1) people interpret the conduct of others by attributing causal explanations to the conduct, such as intentions, temperament, ability or effort, and (2) these causal explanations affect the observer's reactions to the events observed. The causal explanations we tell ourselves tend to fall into two rough categories: dispositional (those factors that are internal to an individual, such as intelligence, motive, or effort) and situational (those factors that are external to an individual, such as luck, task difficulty, or third-party interference).

Attribution processes are essential for making sense of a complex world, but they are prone to cognitive errors of processing or interpretation of perceptions. The first common error is the **fundamental attribution error**, in which we attribute the actions of others to dispositional (internal) causes and attribute our own actions to situational (external) events. (Jones & Nisbett, 1971). Thus, when we see a grammatical or punctuation error in another lawyer's writing, we may attribute it to the lawyer's ignorance or sloppy work habits, but when we make a grammatical or punctuation error, we attribute it to work pressures, or even to our computer's spellcheck function. The fundamental attribution error is powerful. Researchers have shown that "the tendency for attributors to underestimate the influence of situational factors and overestimate dispositional factors in attributing others' behavior is remarkably strong." (Folger, Poole, & Stutman, 2009, p. 60).

The fundamental attribution error is compounded by the second common cognitive error, **the self-serving bias**. As its name suggests, this error describes the tendency of individuals to attribute actions resulting in negative consequences to external factors and attribute positive consequences to internal factors. In other words, we tend to see our successful actions as a function of our internal characteristics and blame failures on situational factors, including the conduct of others. One of the most famous examples of this error is a study examining the explanations of teachers and students for changes on math test scores from one test to another. The teachers consistently attributed improvement to their own teaching ability, but attributed lower scores to the students' ability or effort. The students overwhelmingly engaged in the same self-serving bias, attributing their success to their own effort or intelligence but attributing failures to poor teaching. (Beckman, 1970).

Understanding these common cognitive errors of fundamental attribution error and self-serving bias is important for managing conflict effectively. Because of self-serving bias, people in a conflict frequently attribute the negative consequences of a conflict to the other person. This self-serving bias can heighten bad feelings and resentment toward the other person. The self-serving bias also works in the other direction. People in conflict more often describe their own approaches to managing conflict in positive terms, such as inviting open discussion and avoiding negative judgments of the other person, but characterize the approach of others in the conflict as destructive or manipulative. The fundamental attribution error compounds the difficulty of resolving conflicts, because of our tendency to perceive others' conduct as premeditated and intentional while explaining our own conduct as a reasonable response to the situation. (Folger, Poole, & Stutman, 2009). The fundamental attribution error and self-serving bias arise even when the parties know each other well and, in theory, ought to be more accurate in interpreting each other's actions. Thus, it is no surprise that the frequency of error becomes far greater when the people in collaborative groups do not know each other well or when the conflict occurs between different cultures, genders, or social classes. These errors of perception—errors of attribution—can lead to a vicious cycle in which each party uses the perceived bad conduct of the other party as an excuse for their own negative behavior in the conflict. (Id.).

Some researchers identify the basic "misunderstanding" type of conflict that the "old" goalie and her coach experienced as "pseudo-conflict," because it can often be addressed through careful listening and efforts at clarification, as described below. (Beebe & Masterson, 2003, pp. 260–261). But errors of attribution, such as the fundamental attribution error and self-serving bias, take much more self-awareness and discipline to avoid. Still other conflicts, because they involve fundamental and real differences in goals or actual attempts at interference with another's attempts to achieve specific goals, will persist despite attempts at clarification. Consequently, although clarification strategies are necessary in managing all kinds of conflict, we will consider additional strategies for handling conflict below in the sections on using conflict as a tool and in managing conflict, especially severe conflict.

4.3 · Conflict Styles

Just as cognitive errors can become consistent sources of conflict, people tend to respond to conflict in consistent patterns. (Blake & Mouton, 1964; Hall, 1969; Ruble & Thomas, 1976). It helps to see the range of conflict response styles because, as described above, conflict is a dynamic process. Every party to a conflict has the power to make it better or worse. Recognizing your typical conflict style is important because you can change your conflict style. And you should change your response to conflict—adapting it to the nature of the dispute, the parties to the dispute, the progression of the dispute, and other factors. We will briefly describe and illustrate the five common styles of responding to conflict, then discuss how to think about them as we manage conflict.

Figure 4.1 helps to explain the five common conflict styles: **competing, accommodating, avoiding, compromising** and **problem-solving.** (Thomas, 1976). These patterns have been discussed in some way by virtually every study of conflict management. (Nicotera & Dorsey, 2006). Our discussion here draws primarily from on the work of Professors Joseph P. Folger, Marshall Scott Poole, and Randall Stutman and their excellent book, *Working Through Conflict* (2009). The five common styles are located within two axes, with the vertical axis representing increasing levels of assertiveness (behaviors intended to satisfy self-concerns) and the horizontal axis representing increasing levels of cooperativeness (behaviors intended to satisfy the concerns of others).

Although patterns of conflict can be roughly categorized into these five styles (competing, accommodating, avoiding, compromising and problem-solving), we need to emphasize an important caveat. These styles should not be used as permanent labels to stick on others or yourself. They are patterns of behavior, and behavior can change. The same person may use a variety of styles at different times in different situations with different people, even if that person tends to gravitate toward one or two styles most frequently. Thus, the five styles

Figure 4.1

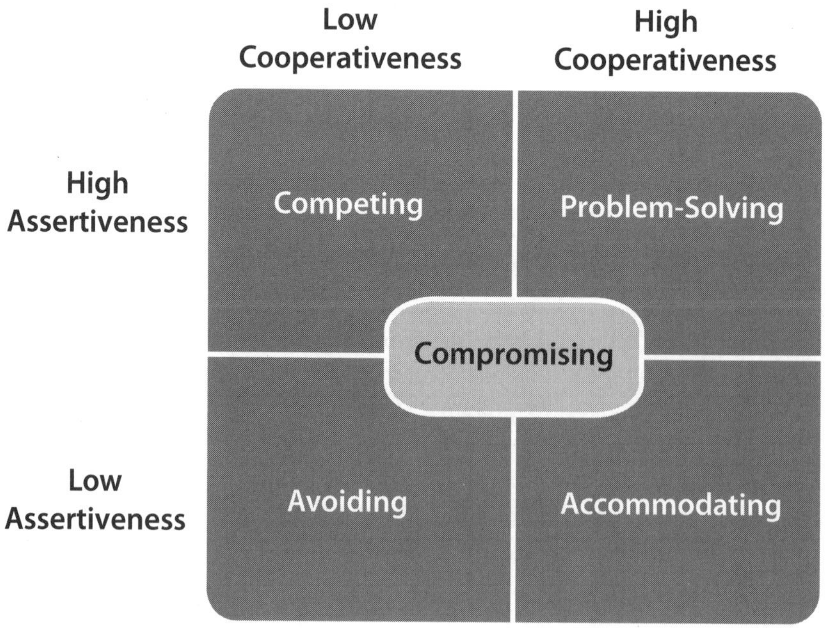

can be used both to describe the typical way a person responds to conflict and to suggest other choices that same person could use to respond to a conflict. You are not "boxed" into a particular style of responding to conflict, no matter how often you resort to it. You always have choices in reacting to conflict.

First, the **competing** style of responding to conflict is characterized by a person's high degree of assertiveness and low degree of cooperativeness. This approach is also called the "dominating" style, since that is how the person tends to behave. This style emphasizes "winning" a dispute at all costs without concern to the other side's perspective or the existence of a future relationship with the other side. An individual with a competitor mindset shows little flexibility and strong effort at controlling the other participants in a dispute.

Researchers identify two sub-types of the competing style. One is "forcing," where the competitor attempts to win the dispute by resorting to sheer superior power, which can manifest itself through rigid demands or highly aggressive physical and verbal conduct. A competitor can also try to win the dispute by using the silent treatment or other manipulative and guilt-inducing behavior. The less intense version of the competing style is "contending." Here, the competitor may be less rigid as long as the competitor ultimately wins. The contending style competitor may also make some effort to explain the competitor's reasons for imposing an outcome on the losing side. In addition, the contending competitor may express some understanding or sympathy for the loser's feelings.

The advantages of the competing approach are efficiency and clarity. People using the competing style to respond to conflict can resolve conflict quickly, imposing clear terms of the resolution. The chief disadvantage of the competing style is that it can breed resentment in others, leading to continued disputes, and inducing others not to cooperate in implementing the resolution to the conflict. Moreover, the individual competitor's actions may threaten effective relationships with others. The competitor may be viewed as less competent and more destructive than people who choose other styles.

The second approach to responding to conflict is the **accommodating** style, which is low in assertiveness and high in cooperativeness. It is sometimes characterized as a "weak" response to conflict because it commonly involves sacrificing one's own interests for the sake of another's interests. Accommodators focus on understanding and providing for the others' needs. The benefit of the accommodating style is that the accommodator's focus on the other party can improve the relationship when the other party feels affirmed and understood. The accommodating style may appear similar to the compromising style, discussed below, because the accommodator believes she is building up "credit" by conceding to the other party, credit that can be traded later for something the accommodator really wants. However, because the accommodator's concession is solely focused on the other party's needs and interests, the accommodator may be disappointed later on to learn that the other party does not feel indebted or grateful and sees no need to reciprocate the accommodator's generosity in a compromise. An accommodator can only ignore her self-interest for a limited time. The accommodator may be left empty-handed and feeling abused when the other party assumes that the accommodator will continue to yield.

The **avoiding** style has some similarity to the accommodating style in that both are low in assertiveness. While accommodators are high in cooperativeness, however, avoiders are low in cooperativeness. Avoiders show little concern for their own interests or the interests of others. Avoiders are characterized by withdrawal, isolation, or refusal to engage. An avoider is often perceived as apathetic, but persons adopting this style may actually be strategic. The person engaged in avoiding behavior is actively preventing others from being able to address the conflict. One variant of the avoiding style is known as "protecting" where a party may go to great lengths to deny the existence of a conflict, even attacking those who try to raise the issues. A less rigid version of the avoiding style is called "withdrawing," where the avoider's tactics are all aimed at keeping the conflict from being addressed directly. To keep the conflict from being addressed directly, the withdrawing avoider may change the subject, insist that the issue is outside the power or jurisdiction of the parties, or demand that the conflict be referred to the proper jurisdiction. The withdrawing avoider may also physically or virtually leave the room, such as by using a smart phone or laptop, or having other excuses for checking out. "Smoothing" is the gentlest form of the avoiding. When smoothing, the avoider dodges issues that create anger or hurt feelings, soothes those negative emotions, and emphasizes common ground, all the while ignoring areas of difference.

The chief benefit of the avoiding style is its ability to buy time. Sometimes parties are not ready to cope with a conflict and the avoider helps the parties get a "time out" before they address it. The weakness of the style is that the conflict is not addressed. Avoiding conflict is not the same as managing or resolving conflict. It can resurface at any time. Because the conflict is not addressed, the parties in conflict may sense a "ticking time bomb" or feel they are "walking on egg-shells." They may be afraid to keep moving forward with a task while the conflict rests barely below the surface. In addition, a party who adopts the avoiding style can frustrate and even anger his significant others or colleagues by disappearing when conflict arises.

The fourth approach is the **compromising** style, often called the "horse-trading" or "sharing" style. As shown in Figure 4.1, the compromising style is located in roughly the center of the assertiveness and cooperativeness matrix. Reciprocity is the key to the compromising style, as it focuses on giving something to get something in return. The compromising style can be modified further as "firm" or "flexible." A firm compromiser will offer a trade-off, criticizing the offer made by the other party but not explaining what she is looking for from the deal. A flexible compromiser is more willing to explore alternative trade-offs and allow the discussion to evolve, disclosing much more of her interests and reasoning—all aimed at her goal of getting the best bargain.

A compromising style has the positive quality of fairness, in the sense that "splitting the difference" is a well-established way to settle a dispute. It can also lead to a relatively quick resolution. However, some compromises are better than others. When the parties have little investment in structuring the best resolution to the conflict for all concerned, the parties may find a low degree of satisfaction with the compromise. A compromiser may perceive that she gave up something she truly valued while in turn she was left with a trade that had little worth to her. That disappointment can develop into bitterness, which can interfere with the compromiser's on-going relationships. Moreover, if a party engages in this style frequently, she may create the expectation that she will always be satisfied with a short-term tradeoff, when that may not be true.

The fifth and final approach to responding to conflict is the **problem-solving** style. Also known as the "collaborative" or "integration" style, the problem-solving style is high in assertiveness and high in cooperativeness. The problem-solver has a "win-win" orientation toward conflict, actively seeking a solution that will meet all parties' most important needs. Of all the conflict styles, conflict management experts most favor the problem-solving style and can be quite effusive in describing its benefits, as illustrated by Professors Folger, Poole and Stutman:

> It can be exhilarating to discover a creative solution through joint effort. Parties learn about themselves and new possibilities open up for the future. These favorable reactions energize people and contribute to effective follow-up and implementation of the solution.

(Folger, Poole & Stutman, 2009, p. 116).

Our experience is that the effective problem solving is indeed uplifting and invigorating. Given this style's benefits, why doesn't everyone use it? The answer is that the problem-solving style to addressing conflict is time-consuming and difficult. Although this style is challenging, we encourage trying it in the right circumstances. We describe the problem-solving style in greater detail in the following section on managing conflict. The key point here is that problem solving takes real commitment to be effective. Sometimes parties engaged in problem solving get so carried away with creativity that their expectations become unrealistic; they become discouraged with the process when proposed solutions are shown to be unworkable. Or sometimes the problem-solving process just takes too long, and parties get frustrated and resort to less effective styles, leaving others with negative impressions of the conflict resolution process.

Finally, remember that conflict is an interactive process involving more than one person. Thus, the problem-solving style is most effective when everyone involved shares this approach. When a party approaches a conflict with a problem-solving orientation, only to be met by an avoider or, even worse, a competitor posing as a collaborator, the problem-solver may be unable to maintain this approach. Moreover, the problem-solver may be harmed by maintaining a positive, win-win approach. Parties using less effective styles may manipulate and take advantage of the problem-solver's goodwill.

It is important to remember that these five styles of responding to conflict are not set in stone. We agree with Professors Folger, Poole and Stutman who argue that the styles should be thought of as "behavioral orientations people can take toward conflict." (2009, p. 108). By this, they mean that individuals have choices about their responses to conflict. Given a particular conflict, they can strategize and alter their behavior. However, Folger, Poole and Stutman also remind us that we cannot approach the process of conflict from the perspective of just one participant.

> The interlocking actions of all parties must be taken into account. Styles represent the "minds-sets" that parties have in the conflict, but what another person does often changes one's attitudes and intentions, often without the individual realizing it. Someone may go into a disagreement with a firm intention to problem solve, but if the other person betrays, or viciously attacks, or refuses to talk about the conflict at all, it is difficult to keep on problem solving. The other's reactions make one want to defend oneself, or strike back, or scream in exasperation or withdraw completely.

(Folger, Poole & Stutman, 2009, p. 109). These researchers are essentially describing the dynamic of many legal collaborations and negotiations. Although many lawyers and law students like to think of themselves as professional problem-solvers, difficult interactions with others can completely dislodge even the most dedicated problem solver from her intended approach.

Conflict management research suggests that while we develop habits of primarily responding to conflict with one or more of these styles, we can change our approaches to conflict as our interactions with others develop. And we need to approach these general orientations to conflict with some caution. Managing conflict is far more complex than identifying a conflict style. The descriptions of conflict styles can be helpful in understanding the benefits and detriments of our common reactions to conflict, but it is more difficult to accurately identify another participant's conflict style. For example, another participant's behavior may appear to be accommodating because the participant appears to be choosing to give up power and control to focus on the needs of the other party. That response, though, can actually be a type of avoiding approach where the avoider gives in rather than risking anger or facing other negative emotional responses from the conflict. Because of this complexity, we recommend that you use the conflict styles as ways of understanding your preferences and seeing options for other approaches. However, when trying to understand someone else's conflict management style, we recommend that you treat the five conflict styles as working hypotheses about the other's preferences and adjust accordingly. Remain sensitive to shifts in the other's behavior so that you can adjust your approach and modify your hypothesis if necessary.

4.4 · Conflict and Cultural and Gender Differences

In responding to conflict, we also need to be cautious about engaging in cultural or gender stereotypes. Being aware of different conflict styles does not mean you can simply assume that certain people will behave in particular ways. Research in intercultural communication suggests that there are significant differences among cultures in approaching conflict. One broad category of cultures, known as "collectivist," are highly aware of context and history, have high degrees of interdependence and a sense of obligation to others. (Hofstede, Hofstede & Minkov, 2010). Collectivist cultures, like those in Japan and Mexico, value the group over the individual. Their communication patterns can be more indirect and subtle, and depend highly on context for meaning. In contrast, "individualist" cultures tend to value individual needs more highly than group needs. The U.S. and Australia are good examples of individualist cultures. In these cultures, communication tends to be direct with participants assuming that meaning is communicated on the surface, independent of situation.

Collectivist and individualist cultures vary in their responses to conflict. One researcher divided these cultures into three approaches or models of conflict—**harmony**, **confrontational**, and **regulative**. (Kozan, 1997). The harmony model is commonly seen in collectivist cultures, which respond to conflict with accommodating and avoiding styles more frequently than other cultures. Within this model, conflict management is aimed more at protecting disruption of the group, and less about protecting the concerns of the individual. In contrast, confrontational cultures accept conflict as necessary. People in these cultures see conflict as a way to further individual needs and goals. They encourage intense expression of emotion and perceive less need to preserve relationships. The third group, regulative cultures, rely more on external factors, such as rules and regulations, to resolve conflict. These cultures emphasize the value of following uniform procedures and using third parties to resolve conflict. (Kozan, 1997).

While collectivist cultures gravitate toward the harmony approach, individualist cultures move toward confrontational or regulative approaches. It is essential to realize, though, that responses to conflict are rough generalizations because conflict styles vary significantly within cultures and subcultures. Cultural conflict styles are best treated as a rudimentary guide until participants can gather enough information to evaluate the conflict response patterns within a particular setting.

Just as it is important not to rely on generalizations about cultural conflict styles, it is equally important to avoid generalizing about conflict style and gender. The concept of "gender" is controversial when we move beyond a biological definition. Moreover, conventional generalizations are usually based on social norms about what is acceptable behavior. In considering gender and responses to conflict, research has shown that women and men use the same kinds of conflict styles. (Folger, Poole & Stutman, 2009; Nicotera & Dorsey, 2006). There is a distinct difference, however, in how women and men are expected to respond to conflict. Women who violate social expectations of conflict styles, such as by using a competing rather than a collaborative or accommodating style, are generally judged more negatively than men who use the same competitor style. (Ivy & Backland, 1994). This is important to keep in mind, as it is dangerous to assume another party's conflict style based on her gender. Instead, use direct observation to develop a working hypothesis about that person's approach to responding to conflict, which can be altered as the person's behavior unfolds.

4.5 · Using Conflict as a Tool

Some conflict within a group is important to the group's success. Without the right amount and type of conflict, a group or team is susceptible to "groupthink." (Janis, 1983). Groupthink is kind of cognitive error that occurs "when a group strives to minimize conflict and reach a consensus without critically testing, analyzing, and evaluating ideas." (Beebe & Masterson, 2000, p. 284). There are several symptoms of groupthink, with the following as warning signs:

- Critical thinking is not encouraged or rewarded;
- Group members are overconfident, thinking they can do no wrong;
- Members engage in stereotyping of "outsiders," characterizing them as incompetent or inferior;
- Members ignore contrary evidence and overvalue supportive evidence, engaging in excessive rationalization;
- Members exert pressure on dissenters and themselves to conform (engaging in self-censorship);
- Members shield their leaders from bad news or contrary information, sometimes becoming what groupthink theorists call self-appointed "mindguards," in that they "guard" the leader from disruptive communication;
- Members are overly concerned with achieving consensus.

A group does not have to show all of these symptoms to suffer from groupthink. Just a few of these behaviors can be so significant that group decision making suffers. (Janis, 1983).

The key to preventing groupthink is to be aware of its signs and to develop a group culture that encourages appropriate kinds of conflict. Building diverse groups in terms of skill sets and personality types helps diminish groupthink; heterogeneous groups are more likely to develop different perspectives and alternatives than homogeneous groups. Group leaders can also strive to encourage critical and independent thinking. Leaders need to be especially aware of their responsibility and influence in helping the group become effective. When a strong or directive group leader expresses enthusiasm for one idea or solution, the remaining group members are far less likely to challenge or critique it. Individual group members can also try to avoid groupthink by minimizing status differences. When all participants perceive themselves on equal footing, they will be more likely to challenge each other. (Street, 1997).

When it is impractical to minimize the power differential among group members, such as in a hierarchical legal organization, it is especially important to adopt specific strategies to encourage criticism and to generate suggestions for alternative solutions. One common technique is to appoint one or more devil's advocates, people who will challenge the ideas of others. In this strategy, after one or more group members present a potential solution, another group member or members have the responsibility to critique it. (Janis, 1989). There are a couple of variants of the devil's advocate approach. With a "dialectical inquiry" approach, one subgroup presents one proposal, while another subgroup presents a counterproposal. Thus each subgroup must both defend its proposal and critique the other group's proposal. (Sims, 1992). A second variant of the devil's advocate is to reserve final judgment until the group has a follow-up meeting. This "second chance" meeting enables group members to review earlier decisions and allows people to raise new concerns or problems. (Janis, 1983, 1989).

Other ways to reduce groupthink are to ask individual group members to vote with private ballots. This approach protects group members who disagree and are unwilling to do so openly or who are fearful of challenging their superiors. Another approach is to ask group members to write down their opinions on a topic before hearing any proposals. Having committed their thoughts to writing, they are often more willing to share them with others. A third approach involves going around the room at a group meeting, asking individual group members to each name their suggestions for solving a problem. Starting with the least senior person in the room, and ending with the most senior, group members are more likely to voice and hear a range of suggestions.

There are two common denominators for preventing and curing groupthink. One is having a group culture that consciously seeks out divergent evidence, opinion, and perspective. A second feature is having a group culture that rewards those who are willing to confront ideas that have widespread support. When a group develops a culture that incorporates this constructive form of conflict, the group members can collaboratively produce better decisions and outcomes than a group that insists on getting along above everything else.

4.6 · Managing Conflict

We now turn to the heart of conflict management. Note that we are talking about managing but not necessarily resolving conflict. We like the metaphor offered by Professors Folger, Poole, and Stutman, who visualize interactive conflict management as a sailboat tacking back and forth in the wind, always aware of changing conditions and adjusting to them. These researchers describe the dynamic of conflict management as an interactive sequence of differentiation and integration. Differentiation occurs as parties express their differences, stake out their positions, and criticize others' positions. Differentiation can go terribly awry if parties retaliate or engage in other forms of negative escalation.

If differentiation is successful, parties emerge with a sense of the others' motives, needs, and values. Successful differentiation also leads parties to recognize other parties' positions, or what they ultimately want for a solution.

Parties probably will not agree with others' positions at this point, but should at least begin to appreciate why the other parties wants what they want.

When differentiation is successful, parties can move toward integration. In the integration phase, the parties refine their appreciation of the others' perspective, generate and analyze potential solutions, commit to a solution, and implement an acceptable solution. Ideally, that solution meets all parties' essential needs; in the alternative, the parties develop a solution that they can live with. (Folger, Poole & Stutman, 2009). As the title of their book, *Working Through Conflict*, suggests, group members should continue to work on identifying solutions to problems when they experience conflict. Group members need not and should not stop because of conflict. The key is to be intentional, flexible, and strategic in managing conflict, making this interactive dynamic work for you instead of against you.

As discussed above, remember to be flexible with your preferred conflict style. Effective conflict management calls for understanding all the styles and knowing when each may be appropriate. Successful conflict management also requires nimbleness, the ability to shift styles in response to the progression of the conflict. Choosing a conflict style at any particular point in time is a function of (1) the importance of the issues to you and others involved in the conflict; (2) the importance of maintaining on-going, positive relationships; (3) situational constraints such as time limitations; and (4) the level of trust among the parties to the conflict. (Folger, Poole & Stutman, 2009).

In describing conflict styles earlier, we noted that problem-solving, or collaboration, is considered the "gold-standard" of conflict styles. Recall, however that the problem-solving approach is not effective in all situations. For example, Professor Linda Putnam's research suggests that using a combination of competing and problem-solving styles may be more effective than using a problem-solving style alone. This combination approach may be more effective because the sharpness of the competing style signals the importance of the issue to the party using it and the competing style communicates the party's resolve. Including features of a competing style also shows that the competing party refuses to be treated as "a pushover," which could increase the costs of the conflict. When parties use this combination approach, they have clearer direction and more incentive to collaborate on a realistic and sustainable solution. (Putnam, 1990). The key, as Professors Folger, Poole, and Stutman put it, is "to differentiate without developing so much negative momentum that spiraling escalation or rigid avoidance occurs." (2009, p. 236).

If you can recognize your "default" conflict style, and understand the importance of recognizing and using other conflict styles that respond to the situation, you can take the next step to managing conflict. Now you need to think about how to frame the problem or conflict. This is a key moment for it can set the stage for a positive problem-solving orientation or for a destructive escalation. In framing the conflict for everyone, it helps to first examine your own perspective. You want to frame the conflict constructively. To do this, recall that we are all prone to attribution error and self-bias, meaning that we tend to overstate others' responsibility and downplay our own. Another requirement is to control your emotions, especially anger and resentment. You also have to be willing to approach the problem from another's perspective, seeking to understand the other party's needs, motivations, and interests as well as you know your own. Finally, work to show respect for the other side at all points during the dispute.

The key to actually framing the dispute effectively is to de-personalize it as much as possible, keeping it focused on cause and effect and avoiding escalating efforts at blaming and shaming. Counter-productive framing can include accusations and exaggerations, such as "You always …" or "That's nuts! That will never work." These kinds of statements are likely to provoke defensiveness and anger. Instead we recommend framing a conflict in this manner: "I have a problem. When you do X, the effect is Y, and I feel Z." (Folger, Poole & Stutman, 2009). An example of a fleshed out version of this formula is: "I have a problem. When we disagree about the answer to one of the quiz questions, your voice gets really loud and intense, which makes others in the group become quiet and less willing to engage in the discussion, including me. I feel intimidated."

The components of effective framing of a conflict or problem are as follows:

(1) **Take ownership of the problem** instead of blaming the other party, which could just invite the party to defend his or her conduct instead of focusing on the problem.
(2) **Describe specific behavior** instead of coloring it with judgmental terms that invite contradiction rather than turning to solutions.
(3) **State the concrete consequences or effects of the behavior.** This helps parties start refocusing on accomplishing the purpose or goal of the interaction.
(4) **Express how the behavior made you feel.** This allows you to express and release difficult emotions without throwing them at the other person. Throwing strong emotions make it difficult or impossible for the other party to see how the party's behavior affects you.

When you frame a dispute, the exact wording is less important than adopting the essential elements above. Using this structure keeps the focus on the problem and its consequences in a way that reduces defensiveness and efforts at blame-shifting. This approach allows the parties to ultimately move forward into generating and evaluating potential solutions.

As you move from the differentiation stage into the integration stage and want to adopt a problem-solving or collaborative style of conflict management, watch out for short-cuts that are introduced to end the dispute. These short-cuts can range from simplistic majority rules votes, coin tosses, and simply giving up to end the conflict. Professors Folger, Poole, and Stutman offer the following additional advice about this fragile point in conflict management. View differences of opinion as normal and helpful rather than as obstacles—differences of opinion can be indications of incomplete information sharing on either side. Differences can also invite the parties to engage in more exploration and communication. Acknowledging and respecting differences also prevent premature resolution or agreement:

- Avoid changing your mind *only to avoid* the conflict and to reach agreement. Withstand pressures to yield that have no objective or logically sound foundation. Strive for enlightened flexibility; avoid outright capitulation.
- Explore the reasons underlying apparent agreements; make sure that people have arrived at similar solutions for either the same basic reasons or for complementary reasons before incorporating such solutions into an agreement or decision.

(Folger, Poole & Stutman, 2009, p. 239)(emphasis in original). Remember that an effective conflict dynamic is interactive rather than linear; parties will move back and forth, from differentiation to integration, to further differentiation and more integration. Slow, steady, and thoughtful progress in managing a conflict beats a fast but fragile and unsatisfying resolution to conflict nearly every time.

4.7 · Coping with Dominators, Free-Riders, Social Loafers, and Other Destructive Behaviors

When people talk about conflicts in teams, they may refer to a specific set of behaviors that harm the group process or are destructive to participants. It is important to develop conflict management strategies so that you feel confident that you can address these situations when they arise. This will enable you to reduce or eliminate these barriers and the resulting group members' resistance to doing productive work. Of course, the best way to handle such behaviors is to prevent them from occurring in the first place. It helps for teams to have mutually agreed upon ground rules or guidelines, preferably in writing. We discuss this more in Chapter Six, where we address the logistics of team work, but it is worth noting here how team guidelines help with destructive behavior. Team guidelines give members of the team something concrete and external to point to when problems arise, making it easier to confront the difficult conduct. For example, if a team has identified "being prepared" as crucial to a team's productive functioning, team members can refer to that guideline when addressing a teammate's unpreparedness. "I have a problem. We agreed earlier that everyone would be prepared when we came to this meeting. When you are unprepared, we don't function efficiently, as we have to spend time reviewing material that everyone else is familiar with. This makes me really frustrated." When the problems do occur, the conflict management process discussed above, including identifying an effective style and framing the conflict constructively, can serve as an overarching framework.

In this final section on conflict, we want to offer additional concrete suggestions for the most frequent complaints about difficult individuals in groups and teams: members who "dominate" others or members who are "slackers" or "social loafers." We describe several specific interventions your group can take for these problematic behaviors, but have a few general tips first. Approach any problematic behavior with this understanding—you are more likely to succeed at changing someone's behavior than at changing the person. Thus, keep the focus on the problematic individual's behavior and the observable consequences of that behavior. As we advised above, avoid making comments about the person's character or abilities. Intervene as soon as the problem behavior surfaces—do not just hope it goes away on its own. Finally, when you need to discuss the situation with the member whose behavior is a problem, one or more of the group members should have the conversation with the individual at a time and place where there is adequate privacy.

First, let's consider the problem of dominating behavior. Identify the offensive behavior—what do you see or hear? Is the person refusing to listen to others in the group, interrupting them, or cutting off discussion? Is the person asserting opinions without having any authority or evidence for them and insisting that she is correct? The team's response to the dominator depends on the specific behavior. If the dominator constantly interrupts others, then team members need to respond by immediately identifying the interruption. If you are interrupted, interject immediately by saying, "Hang on—I'm not finished talking yet." If someone else is interrupted, respond immediately by saying, "Wait, I want to hear the rest of what Chelsea is saying." Sometimes it helps to emphasize the verbal message using a universal nonverbal signal—hold up your hand as a "stop" sign.

If the teammate's problematic behavior is dominating the team's discussion time, one specific response is to set a guideline for discussion such as no one speaks for more than two minutes, or no one speaks twice in a row unless no one else wants to speak. For someone who is too assertive or conclusory, the best intervention is to neutrally ask for that person's evidence, supporting material, or reasoning. "That's an interesting idea. I'm not familiar with the evidence in support of that suggestion. Could you help me better understand the support for this approach?" It is important to understand that dominators may be as heavily invested in the team's success, but not have good personal or communication skills. It is best to first try approaching dominators as if they are well-intentioned, rather than just bullies. Of course, some dominators may well be bullies, in which case they might respond to your intervention with verbal attacks or threats. In that situation, see the discussion below on dealing with more severe problems.

Like dominators, free-riders, social loafers, and slackers come in different varieties. As suggested earlier, first identify the specific problematic behavior. Does the person listen to the discussion but not contribute to it? Is the person actively disengaged in the group because the slacker is doing other things like checking e-mail, Facebook, playing solitaire, or daydreaming? Is the person late to meetings or unprepared when he does appear? Address the specific behavior. When a person is attentive but unusually quiet, give her time to process the information in the group discussion, then directly ask for her input. "Grace, how do you think we should respond to this client?"; "Grace, you've had some experience with this client, what do you think about the approach that is being suggested?" As we discussed in Chapter Two, while some people are eager to talk, others hesitate in sharing ideas. Sometimes this is because the individual is an introvert. Other people may be unsure that they have anything to add or are concerned that others are not interested in their views. Sometimes individuals do not participate because of cultural differences or differences in social power. The safest course here is not to assume the individual is deliberately withholding information—just expressly invite and encourage the person to share information and ideas.

For the slacker who has checked out of the group, make it harder for him to virtually leave the group. Often people who check out in this manner do not see their behavior as problematic. In a sense, they think they are invisible. Their behavior is reinforced when members of teams are more than happy to let others not participate. To respond to the person who has checked out, make sure she knows she is visible. Create and enforce a group ground rule that members will not check e-mail, text, or surf the web during group meetings.

The same principle applies for the slacker who is chronically late or unprepared. Identify the behavior and the consequences it has for the group. If the problematic behavior continues, the group may need to protect itself by reshaping each member's responsibilities so as to contain the damage that the irresponsible member's conduct can cause the group. The group can also revisit any previous guidelines. It may be that the members of the team have different perspectives on what it means to be prepared or on time. By revising their guidelines team members can refine them to be more specific, e.g., "Being on time means that everyone is present and ready to discuss items on the agenda by the time the meeting officially starts."

Suppose, however, that the behavior your group encounters is really problematic, and here we mean serious anger issues, bullying, or unethical or bigoted behavior. This is a team member's worst nightmare. The good news is that, with some modifications, the basic conflict management process described above can help here. However, it is essential that the team address the highly destructive behavior together. A collaborative, whole team approach is considerably more effective than one individual's attempt to address the destructive actions. The power of social approval is very strong, even with borderline pathological behavior, and can be used to influence behavioral changes productively.

When a team member's actions are extreme, the problem-solving style of conflict management is not likely to work. A skillful and destructive individual can often abuse or manipulate the most effective problem-solver to his own advantage. The more productive approaches are likely to be combinations of the competing and avoiding or accommodating/smoothing style. When using the competing approach, members of the team emphasize confronting their teammate directly about the teammate's destructive behavior. Here, the team uses its collective power and authority to let the individual know the problematic behavior will not be tolerated. These confrontations can be combined with the smoothing style, where members of the team reinforce common goals and interests, and seek to understand their teammate's underlying emotions. Depending on the team dynamics, the entire team can adopt these approaches or some of the team members can do the confrontation work, while others do the smoothing. The team must take care not to allow the troubled team member to drive a wedge between the other members. However, as long as the team is united in its goal of stopping the unacceptable behavior of their teammate, this "good cop/bad cop" approach can be effective.

With bullying, unethical, or bigoted conduct, the basic methods still apply. The most effective approach is to have the team collectively focus on the specific behavior that is unacceptable and explain the undesirable consequences for the group and the feelings it engenders for individuals and the group. Finally, teammates must insist that the destructive behavior ceases. If the destructive behavior does not stop, members of the team may need to engage in avoidance, isolating the troublesome individual. In organizations, it is frequently better to refer unethical, bigoted, or bullying behavior to human resources, the supervisor of the work group, or professor in a classroom setting than to try further attempts at changing the behavior with the group. In other situations, teammates should work together to first try to change the behavior.

When team members engage in inappropriate displays of anger, other members of the team have an even greater need to be able to shift conflict styles. Anger or intense outbursts call for an asymmetrical response. Members should communicate in a calm and slow manner, using a low volume. This response is smoothing verbal behavior and can de-escalate intense emotions. Sometimes it helps to acknowledge the anger and even apologize for setting off the volatile response, as a way of allowing the destructive team member to have time to regain emotional stability. When destructive behavior is acknowledged in this way, team members should not state or suggest that the response was justified. Instead, they acknowledge that something provoked the anger, and that their teammate experiences real anger.

Another way to diffuse the tension is to calmly but attentively ask the angry individual for information, what, from that person's perspective, ignited the angry response? Paraphrase the individual's response to buy more time and to communicate that you are actively listening. In the rare case where there is any concern about the physical or emotional safety or well-being of those in the group, the best strategy is to withdraw or disengage from the problem member, postponing any discussion until it can resume in a calm fashion or until others can be consulted.

Applications

1. Think about three different conflicts you have had. For each conflict, identify what might have caused the conflict, how the conflict was responded to, and how the situation ended.
2. Considering different conflicts you have been involved with, identify your preferred style of responding to conflict.
3. Does your preferred style of conflict management change depending on the situation? If so, when and how does it change?
4. Overcoming the self-serving bias. Think of a time when you have experienced your greatest success. Think about what you did and how you

prepared to reach your accomplishment. Now, try to remove yourself from the accomplishment; that is, try to redistribute the credit for the success to others who contributed. Does it come easily? Had you recognized these contributions before?

5. Role-Play. In pairs, take on the role of either Accuser or Responder. The Accuser starts the role-play by accusing the Responder of something, such as trying to steal a client, talking negatively about the Accuser with a superior, or not contributing sufficiently to a team. Be creative in your accusations! The Accuser can play this however the Accuser would like (intense and forward, passive aggressive, etc.). The Responder's task is to try to defuse the situation. Keep in mind the principles laid out in this chapter. In particular, remember that you are *managing* the conflict, don't necessarily try to find a resolution right away.

6. Suppose the following people are on your team:
    a. Ted: Brings attention to his own expertise at every chance; uses sarcasm to put others down.
    b. Claire: Hilariously funny, she makes everyone laugh but often gets the team off the agenda and interrupts the work flow.
    c. Nancy: New to the team, came from a foreign branch office. She has no language difficulties, but says nothing during meetings.
    d. Eric: Smart guy, but tries to do as little work as possible; often late to team meetings.
    e. David: Regularly takes at least fifteen minutes of the team's time to talk about his problems with his teenage daughter, who is in a serious rebellion phase.

What information would you like to have about these individuals? If you had that information, what would you do to address their behavior?

Chapter 5

Making Decisions in Groups and Teams

5.1 · The Importance of Deciding How to Decide

"Lawyers and policy makers regularly serve as the leaders of decision-making groups. The leader's role is key in harnessing the power of groups and in preventing the pitfalls that attend group decision-making." (Brest & Krieger Hamilton, 2010, p. 627).

Wayne, a senior associate at a large firm, was pulled into a large, highly specialized project only days before it was due. He noted that senior attorneys knew about the project, could have seen the looming deadline, but somehow very little was done. Suddenly five other associates and three partners were in crisis mode. "It's like a fire drill, where you are throwing bodies out the window." Work was divided up according to whom could do what, not based on any design or plan. It was unclear to Wayne who was working on what part, or how the parts would come together. "I don't know who's in charge. We have 48 hours to file all these documents, and no one has talked about who has the master document."

As is shown by Wayne's story, a decision can be the end, the beginning, or even a transition or midpoint in a team's work, but the process of decision-making is generally the key task of most work groups. Professors Brest and Krieger Hamilton observe that "Lawyers and policy makers regularly serve as the leaders of decision-making groups. The leader's role is key in harnessing the power of groups and in preventing the pitfalls that attend group decision-making." (2010, p. 627).

Some theorists draw a distinction between decision-making and problem-solving, but we will use the terms interchangeably because the concepts are difficult to separate in practice. We will offer a classic, flexible framework for decision-making and describe some of the most common problems groups encounter in reaching decisions. However, the central point of this chapter is this: it matters less which decision-making process your group decides to follow than that your group follows a decision-making process. Wayne observed hasty reaction without reflection, and everyone in the firm paid a price for that lack of a decision-making process. In general, teams make better decisions when they choose and follow an agreed upon and explicit structure for problem solving. (Hirokawa & Scheerhorn, 1986).

Yet it is often difficult for a group to make "deciding how to decide" a top priority.

Legal professionals—including law students working in groups—frequently work under pressure with tight time constraints like Wayne's firm. The temptation in this situation is to plunge right into the task, with all group members flailing away at the problem in the hope of reaching a solution. In this pressure-cooker, many feel there is no time to "waste" on planning or process, especially if it means that planning requires coordinating communication among many participants. "Crisis" or "crunch time" will lead group members to quickly divide up the tasks to get them done. You can probably predict the outcome of this story—some of the people did the work assigned, some did not, and a great deal of energy was expended unproductively. Of those who did the work, some of them put a lot of energy and thought into it, others did not. In the best situations, one person takes over the mess and tries to put something coherent together by the group's deadline. In the worst situations, like Wayne's observations, the end product is a mish-mash of slap-dash effort for which no one in the group wants to take responsibility.

Truly chaotic or crisis situations may not allow time to create a process for decision-making. A genuine work crisis will call for a rapid response. Because of the urgency, the decision is likely to be a top-down directive from the group's leader. Several problems arise from this top-down approach to decision-making. First, to work effectively, the leader must communicate clearly and directly with all team members, so that each team member understands his or her role and can respond appropriately. This level of strong leadership is rare, but it does occur. Second, crisis decision-making is accompanied by high stress for the leader and the team. Organizations can function for a while under these conditions, but a breakdown is inevitable. Third, this approach allows for little to no input from the team, which results in missed opportunities for creative solutions provided by a diverse group of individuals.

Finally, some lawyers are consciously or unconsciously tempted to define most problems as crises because members of the group believe that they are more productive that way. The adrenaline rush of crisis management can be addictive for both the leader and the team even if, like many addictions, it is ultimately unproductive, if not destructive. Thus, the first step for any effective decision-making is to take a deep breath and make a realistic assessment: is this a true crisis or a serious problem to solve? Planning a process for decision-making requires time, and it is worth the investment for a chance at a better final product. The more serious the problem, the more valuable a process can be. It may even change what appeared to be a crisis into a less urgent problem. Having some breathing room will allow all involved to likely make better decisions and reduce the risk of errors.

Some caveats are appropriate. First, a good process does not guarantee a good decision. In discussing conflict management, we discussed the danger of cognitive errors or biases, the mental mistakes we all make in processing information and drawing conclusions. We all tend to make these errors especially when judging our own behavior or the behavior of others. These individual cognitive errors can be compounded by the group process, creating frustration and failure. However, groups that choose and follow a thoughtful process can minimize cognitive errors in decision-making. (Hirokawa & Scheerhorn, 1986). A particular group may need more or less structure, depending on the group members' abilities and the nature of the task. Nevertheless, some structure is essential to keep any group focused and effective.

Second, although we talk about following a decision-making process, we do not mean to suggest that decision-making is a purely linear process. We list steps or stages in decision-making, but any good decision-making process is iterative and recursive. This means that you will sometimes revisit previous steps in the process after realizing you need more information or missed a potential alternative that should be evaluated before reaching a final decision. Backtracking to previous steps does not mean the process has failed. Even though the iterative process may feel like you are spending too much time or energy on one phase, it can also signal that you and your group are critically evaluating and improving your work as you go along. You are using each other and the process to generate better product than you could as an individual.

Finally, we are not attempting to provide a complete catalogue of approaches to decision-making and problem solving. The best teams adapt their approaches to the complexity of the situations they face. (Snowden & Boone, 2009). Strong leadership is always essential. For example, on a high-level clinic team, which included both high functioning students and lawyers as well as important law firm attorneys, a strong quarterback was set up from the start. The strong leader model allowed everyone on the team to relax and defer to the leader on all issues of importance. The individual strengths then came through.

The key is that once a crisis ends, a good team will analyze the lessons learned from the experience and incorporate them in their process. Here, we offer you tools and tips to adapt to your group's specific purposes, but this is not an exhaustive list. In our bibliography, we try to provide you with the best work we have found, and encourage you to keep reading and building your decision-making tools. We now turn to a classic flexible framework for group decision-making.

5.2 · Getting Started with Dewey's Reflective Thinking Process: The Standard Agenda

One of the leading American intellectuals of the 20th century, John Dewey was a psychologist, educator, political philosopher, and social critic. In his book, *How We Think*, Dewey identified a process for effective decision making or problem solving. (Dewey, 1910). This process is called the Reflective Thinking model, which some researchers call the Standard Agenda. Figure 5.1 shows the basic stages of Dewey's model.

Figure 5.1

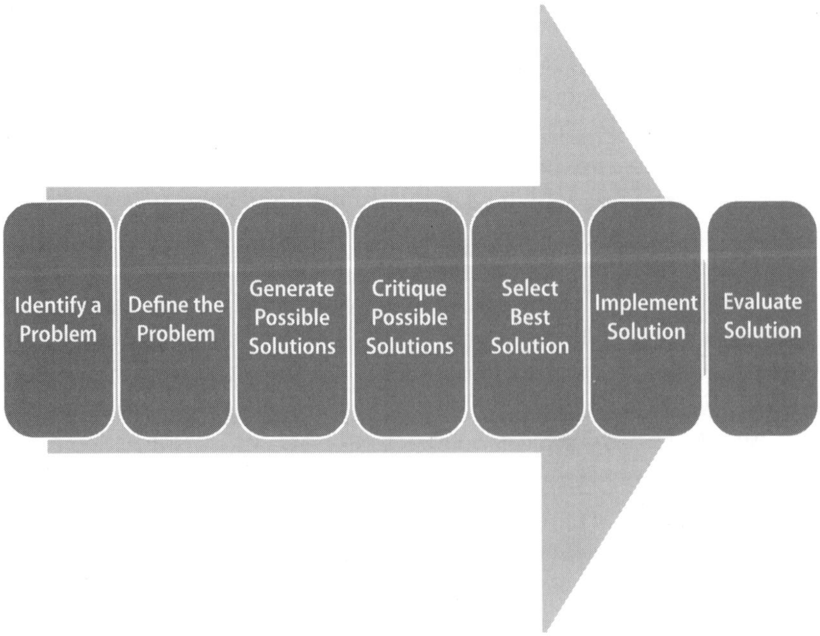

Dewey's classic Reflective Thinking model has been adapted repeatedly by management consultants, scholars, and practitioners. Other approaches to problem solving are all variations on the Reflecting Thinking model, and a testament to it being a foundational and flexible decision-making framework.

In Chapter Three, we saw the need for a group to clearly identify and define its goals or objectives. The initial stages of the Reflective Thinking process show that a team may still need to spend time clarifying the nature of the problem that the members of the team have been given to solve. A checklist of initial questions to use in structuring a discussion to identify and analyze a problem also provides an outline for seeking necessary initial data or information.

(1) What terms or phrases do we need to define so we know we are talking about the same thing?
(2) Who is affected by the problem?
(3) Where does the problem occur?
(4) When does the problem occur?

Sometimes the usefulness of this checklist can be expanded if you reverse the questions:

(1) What terms or phrases do we agree we understand?
(2) Who is not affected by the problem?
(3) Where does the problem not occur?
(4) When does the problem not occur?

Answers to these questions can help to define the scope and ramifications of the problem, as well as help the group distinguish among symptoms of a problem and actual causes of a problem.

5.3 · Generating Criteria and Ideas for Possible Solutions

Rachel works in a newly created interdisciplinary department of a large public agency. She and her colleagues are excited about making changes in the agency, but they have faced resistance from others who had been working for the agency a long time. When seeking funds to accomplish a project, Rachel learned the hard way that she could not just submit a request and expect others to help. Instead, she would be required to go through every bureaucratic hurdle. After her first request for funding was denied, she had to dig around to find out why. She was told she needed to complete certain forms. Only after she had completed and submitted a new request did she learn that she needed to complete the forms differently. This happened several times, much to Rachel's frustration. She realized though, that it would be more effective to learn about and work with the bureaucracy than to point out the senselessness of the procedures. Now, whenever submitting a request for funding, she always first finds out what forms are needed, what checklists are available, and what samples she can review, so that she has everything with her up front. "It may take ten minutes to talk to the relevant people and make sure I have all the forms and samples and checklists, but it is much more efficient later."

This simple example of the adjustment to organizational processes (more pejoratively called bureaucracy) highlights how the process of identifying and defining a problem may overlap with the next stages, responding with and critiquing possible solutions. Groups do a better job in the later stage of evaluating potential solutions if they generate criteria for solutions before they begin to generate possible solutions. (Beebe & Masterson, 2003; Rothwell, 2004). We begin by suggesting several basic criteria that can be used as a template for discussing a group's preferences—applicability, practicality, desirability.

5.3.1 · Generating Criteria for Solutions: Questions of Applicability, Practicality, and Desirability

Before developing actual solutions or potential decisions, the team should list its criteria for the best decision. Sometimes the criteria for the best solution can come from a well-crafted mission and vision statement. For example, in 2012, the faculty of William Mitchell College of Law was asked to vote to adopt a resolution to oppose a controversial proposed amendment to the state constitution. Decision-making in such a large, diverse, and critical group was daunting. Moreover, several faculty members initially expressed concern that speaking out on a controversial issue involving the state constitution was beyond the scope of the faculty's jurisdiction. To respond to this concern, the advocates of the resolution framed the decision in terms of the values the law school had adopted in its mission and vision statements. The mission of the school is "We serve the law. We study it, practice it, and work to make it just." (For the full version, see http://www.wmitchell.edu/about/mission.html). Any decision on the proposed resolution had to meet this standard—would it be consistent with (1) our educational and pragmatic work with law and (2) our objective of making the law more "just?" In light of those criteria, a strong majority of the faculty ultimately decided to pass the resolution to the proposed constitutional amendment. A simpler example can happen every time two students work together, but really work separately, as the next example illustrates.

On a clinical case, two students split the issues on a brief and wrote them separately then exchanged drafts for critique. One student totally rewrote the other's work in the process while the other student did not comment at all. They did not discuss evaluative criteria in advance so neither student expected this level of feedback. The students stopped talking to each other, told the clinician they hated each other, and had to be assigned to other teams on other projects.

Not all organizations have criteria and not all teams are given criteria. Furthermore, the criteria given may not be appropriate for some decisions. To fill the need in those situations, you can use a well-established template of topics to generate criteria. Current or former debaters may recognize these topics, derived from rhetorical theory: applicability, practicality, and desirability. The questions below summarize the topic areas and provide examples of key questions to pose within each area to help stimulate discussion of criteria for effective decisions and solutions.

Applicability: questions that address how well a solution fits the problem.

(1) Will the solution solve the entire problem?
(2) Does the solution address the cause(s) of the problem?
(3) If the solution addresses only part of the solution, will it address the bulk of the problem or does it leave a significant part of the problem unresolved?

Practicality: questions that address the feasibility of putting the solution to work.

(1) How long will the solution take?
(2) How expensive will the solution be?
(3) What other resources will be required for the solution to work (other personnel, teams, stakeholders)?
(4) Are the time, financial, and other resources available?
(5) What unintended consequences may result from the decision?
(6) Will such consequences be more troublesome than the original problem?
(7) Does the solution account for other barriers to implementation (such as lack of information, biases, hostility to change, or attitudinal problems)?

Desirability: questions that address the ethics and values of the team, both as a whole and as individuals.

(1) Will the solution further the mission or values of the team?
(2) Will the solution harm anyone—psychologically, economically, physically, socially, or spiritually?
(3) Will individual members of the team be uncomfortable with the ethics of the solution?

(4) Is the solution consistent with the text of any code of ethics that the team must follow (such as the Student Conduct Code, or state bar Rules of Professional Responsibility relevant for attorneys)?

(5) Is the solution consistent with the spirit of any code of ethics that the team must follow?

Just identifying this rubric to clinical students at the start of each semester could save countless hours of time otherwise wasted in uncertainly, emotional turmoil, or other unproductive activity.

5.3.2 · Generating Ideas for Possible Solutions

The most creative part of problem solving and decision-making comes when group members imagine possible solutions.

On every case, clinicians take time just to brainstorm the issues and strategy with the students because inevitably the range of experiences and perspectives always results in a new idea. At a brainstorming session on a wrongful conviction case, the students suggested that they act out and film the prosecutor's version of how the accused committed the crime. While the attorneys would never have thought to do this, the resulting investigation established the impossibility of the prosecutor's version of events.

Creativity and innovation have been identified as one of the essential 26 characteristics of a successful lawyer. (Shultz & Zedeck, 2011). Nevertheless, not everyone views the terms "creativity" and "imagination" positively. Some lawyers may cringe at the suggestion, thinking of chaotic and haphazard discussion. Such reactions come from a lack of experience with a good process for developing ideas.

The most popular technique for generating possibilities in a group is brainstorming. First discussed in advertising, brainstorming is a way to emphasize imaginative solutions in problem solving, instead of focusing solely on evaluation and critique. Sadly, most of us have never engaged in really good brainstorming sessions. At its most raw form, we know that brainstorming involves a group of individuals throwing out ideas at random, while a couple of people try to keep track of all of them. Brainstorming can be an effective process when a few basic principles are followed. We have compiled here a list of brainstorming best practices. (Beebe & Masterson, 2003; Lumsden, Lumsden & Wietoff, 2010; Rothwell, 2004). These principles are easy to state, but may be hard for analytical and critical thinkers to follow. These guidelines are worth a try, however, because they will improve even the most basic brainstorming session.

Preparing for Brainstorming

Understand how brainstorming fits within your problem solving or decision-making process. We have suggested Dewey's classic Reflective Thinking process and discussed developing criteria that any solution would have to satisfy. It is challenging to combine these analytical techniques with the more organic brainstorming approach. The solution criteria in group members' minds create evaluative and critical roadblocks to the creative possibilities generated during a good brainstorming session. If you plan to use brainstorming, then you may want to defer generating criteria for a solution until you reach the evaluative stage. You may need to instruct members of the group on ways to free their minds from some natural constraints such as budgetary, personnel, other logistics, and even deadlines. If the time frame is short, then the problem-solving process can be truncated to

(1) define the problem;
(2) brainstorm solutions; and
(3) evaluate and pick one solution to try.

For example, in one group of lawyers, the group would brainstorm solutions by starting the session with the phrase "If money and time were no object, how would we ... ?"

Be sure each member of the group understands the problem. This may seem rather obvious, but the failure of many brainstorming sessions results from an unclear description of the problem. If the problem is complex, you will want to provide the team with the problem statement in advance. Recall from Chapter Two that introverts generally appreciate having time to think about issues before they speak. Although research may be part of a group's process for analyzing the problem, some individuals may want or need to do research to stimulate their thinking.

Be sure everyone understands why you are using brainstorming, as well as the rules for the brainstorming session and their rationales. Research shows that brainstorming can produce more ideas and better ideas, but only if the participants understand the process and follow the guidelines for effective brainstorming. (Firestein, 1990).

Set a time limit for the brainstorming session, but do not make it too short. This is a good place to consult the team. One possible technique is to set an overall time frame, but have a numerical goal in mind: "We will quit at 4 p.m. or when we reach 50 ideas, whichever comes first."

Limit the group size for oral brainstorming sessions. The larger the group size, the more likely that some members will not participate and the more difficult it is to enforce the rules. If a large group (beyond five members) is required, the leader may want to consider the nominal group or Delphi techniques discussed below.

Guidelines for Conducting a Brainstorming Session

Do not evaluate ideas while brainstorming. This first commandment of brainstorming is routinely broken. Lawyers, law professors, and law students seem particularly prone to responding with critique or in the best circumstances saying, "yes, but." This is understandable; lawyers practice thinking analytically and critically. For a brainstorming session, though, try hard to hold each other back from any kind of interpretative or evaluative comments. It is often easier to adjust or revise an idea later than to think one up in the first place. And remember that nonverbal communication is communication; watch out for caustic tone of voice, eye-rolling, head shaking, or other signals of disapproval.

Follow the guidelines. Group leaders should remind members of the guidelines, obtain members' agreement to follow them, and enforce them. If group members persist in breaking the rules after being reminded to stop, Professors Beebe and Masterson suggest asking the offending members to record the ideas of others; it is harder to talk when you must listen carefully and write accurately. They also suggest that if this continues to be a problem, the group or team leader may need to consider an alternative to standard oral brainstorming, such as described below. (Beebe & Masterson, 2003).

Do not clarify and do not ask for clarification of an idea. Asking for clarification or detail can turn into a rendering a judgment and can slow down the creative process such that the next potential speaker reconsiders. The time to seek clarification is once the brainstorming ends. In the brainstorming process, the facilitator must try to keep the atmosphere positive and accept each idea in its best, most workable light.

Piggyback on others' suggestions. There is no concept of intellectual property in the brainstorming context. If one idea does not seem feasible, you should let someone else suggest an iteration. No one owns an idea — everyone is responsible for building the ideas.

Write down only the ideas, not who offered them. The idea keeps the focus on possible solutions, rather than allowing group members to be distracted by personality or status issues among members of the groups.

Everyone has to contribute something. No idea is off limits or too impractical for this generative stage. If some members of the group are silent, one of the last steps is to ask explicitly for their ideas. You might remember from the discussion of personality and preferences in Chapter Two that extroverts are often eager to share their ideas. Introverts, however, need some quiet time to think about or process their thoughts before they feel comfortable sharing them. The Myers Briggs Type Indicator also offers an ironic addition to brainstorming; some introverts are uncomfortable with sharing undeveloped ideas. Thus, self-consciousness about brainstorming might be a trained response in some people. Recognizing this response, and having a facilitator emphasize that the goal of the session is to air half-baked ideas, may help introverts develop greater comfort in expressing their perspectives. While brainstorming is easy and fun for extroverts, giving the team advance notice that a particular meeting will be devoted to brainstorming allows introverts to think about the issues in advance and feel as comfortable in the process. At a minimum, you can set aside a few minutes for quiet thought before asking any group to launch into the process.

Variations on Basic Brainstorming Sessions

A great deal of research has explored the dynamics of brainstorming and resulted in several variants, some of which are designed to use the wisdom of the team while drawing on the benefits of individual accountability. The Nominal Group Technique is especially helpful if you have a group dominated by introverts, who may spend more of the discussion time listening to the ideas of others instead of contributing their own. This technique can also be helpful if you are concerned about some group members slacking because they are less engaged or committed to the decision-making process than others. In general, the basic brainstorming process can make it easy for these individuals to hide. While some mistakenly think these participants are laid back or lazy, these individuals each have a different perspective and have something to offer. This variant of the brainstorming process holds them accountable. The Nominal Group Technique process is as follows:

- The problem has been defined and analyzed to a high degree; each group member can explain the situation.
- Working individually, group members write down every possible solution they can generate.
- Each group member reports the solutions that person has generated, one at a time. The ideas should be visually reported—on a white board, or an electronic board so that everyone can see the ideas.
- Group discussion follows, aimed at clarifying the ideas, not critiquing or judging them.
- After discussing all of the ideas, each group member ranks the solutions, with a "1" being the most effective solution in the individual's opinion. If there are many ideas, group members can rank their top

five. The top solutions, the ones with the lowest scores, are tabulated and identified.

- The group then discusses the rankings. If the group does not like the outcome, there can be additional discussion to clarify the proposals or raise concerns or other observations. Then the group can re-rank the remaining solutions to see if there is any stronger consensus.

Despite using a ranking system to prioritize solutions, the Nominal Group Technique process is not directed at picking a particular solution by voting. We discuss methods of making final decisions in groups below, and voting is one option, but it is seldom the best option. The idea behind the Nominal Group Technique and ranking is to engage both individual resources and the benefits of group dynamics to generate and sort serious solutions to a problem or to identify the most viable option(s).

The **Delphi Technique**, named after the location of the ancient Greek oracle who dispensed the wisdom of Apollo, is also called absentee brainstorming because it can be used through email or platforms to accommodate distance. This technique is not only used where face-to-face meetings are not logistically practical, but also where tension or conflict is running high in a group or where other reasons such as status differences make anonymous contributions valuable in the process. Here are the Delphi technique's key elements:

- The group leader serves as the "oracle" in the Delphi technique. The leader distributes a written statement of the problem to be solved or decision to be made, and invites group members to provide individual solutions or ideas.
- The group members generate responses individually and submit them to the leader.
- The leader summarizes all of the individual responses without identifying their source, and asks for additional reactions, ideas, and suggestions.
- The leader then summarizes the additional reactions, ideas, and suggestions and shares that summary with the group.
- The process of seeking group input can continue, if the leader thinks it is necessary, or the leader can ask the individuals to rank order the solutions or ideas and return those to the leader.
- Eventually, group feedback and rankings help the leader find the consensus about the most promising solutions.

The key benefits of the Delphi technique are that it both provides individual accountability and maintains anonymity to neutralize potential issues related to bias, social conformity, and source bias. It also allows the group process to take place when individuals are scattered in different locations. The biggest downsides are that it is time-consuming, puts a large burden on the leader to summarize and disseminate the information, and requires a high degree of trust that the leader is not filtering information. Moreover, the technique does not allow for spontaneous creativity that can result from hearing the ideas of others.

One common challenge throughout these techniques is balancing individual contributions with the creativity and energy that comes from group interaction and sharing. The **Stepladder Technique**, which seeks to do so, staggers the involvement of individuals in the process to elicit their contributions of information, solutions, and ideas while they are still relatively independent of the team. The Stepladder Technique then has individuals share that information in a way that enables the team to build on the ideas. The process proceeds accordingly:

- Each member of the team has time to reflect on the problem.
- Two members of the team discuss the problem and their preliminary ideas for resolving the problem.
- New members enter the team one at a time. The new member must present his or her idea before hearing what the other team members have said.
- The team then discusses all of the proposals before the next team member enters.
- The team repeats this process until all team members have been heard in this process, only then does the team move to choose a solution.

Regardless of which variation of brainstorming the group uses, it is important for the leader to explain what will happen to the ideas generated in the session. Most of us have had the bad experience of investing significant effort in helping groups generate ideas in an organization, either informally or at a retreat, only to see the product filed away and never seen or discussed again. Ideally, a good brainstorming session leads to either an evaluative and selection stage of the problem solving or decision-making. It is incumbent upon the organizer of the session to affirm the value of the process and the best way to do so is through sharing the next steps.

5.4 · Evaluating and Selecting the Best Ideas or Solutions

Step Back. Dewey's Reflective Thinking model may look linear, however, as noted earlier, decision-making is really a series of cycles. After attempting to brainstorm potential solutions, a group may decide that its members do not truly understand or agree on the definition of the problem and go back to work on that stage. Reconsidering potential solutions could come from other forces, such as fact changes, additional leadership insight, and change in the law.

Selecting the most effective solutions after initially brainstorming ideas frequently leads a group to return to the drawing board. As a result, selecting the best solutions can be difficult. By this point, the group can often see the stakes involved with a potential decision and that brings unnecessary stress to the process. Even if the group has a positive problem or good stress, such as deciding who among some talented individuals should be hired, the process is draining. A lot of individual and group time has been invested in the process. Sub-groups or factions may have started to coalesce around particular alternatives, potentially increasing conflict within the group. Individual egos can attach to one or more ideas, reducing the critical analysis ability of those individuals.

We want to remind you that returning to an earlier step in the process is not a sign of failure. Revisiting earlier stages of a conscious process is a sign of the thoroughness of the participants and the process. As we note in the Preface, revisiting an earlier step familiar to us; during the years we worked on this book, we revisited and retraced our steps many times. We know how frustrating a group process can be. With resolve, though, we continued forward, because we believed in both the process and the goal.

See and Study All the Options. In evaluating potential solutions, the team must physically see them. To see the possibilities it is best if the choices are visible to everyone at the same time, together. Then figure out how to record the evaluation. Law students are often taught to analyze or argue legal issues from both sides. Some of us instead ask students to look beyond the simple two sides approach and consider all sides of a legal dispute. If you take a bifurcated approach to evaluating the possible solutions, use a simple T Chart, with "pros" as the heading of one side and "cons" on the other.

Figure 5.2 · T Chart

Pro	Con

For more complex evaluation, you should use a decision matrix or grid, organized as a table, with options on one axis and criteria on the other, as in Figure 5.3.

Figure 5.3 · Example Decision Matrix

Options	Criterion 1	Criterion 2	Criterion 3
Candidate A	Yes	No	Yes
Candidate B	Yes	Yes	Yes
Candidate C	No	No	Yes

Many other ways will help to visualize a team's possible decisions. Our point here is that most people need to see, as well as hear, the analysis.

Advantages, Disadvantages and Risks. If a couple of options satisfy all the relevant criteria, you might find yourself first using a matrix, then subjecting those options to an additional T Chart, labeled advantages/disadvantages, for each option. In this common scenario, once you have that list you will want to consider applying further questions like these:

- Do the advantages flow inevitably from this option, or do they require other actions to be realized?
- Are the disadvantages unavoidable, or can the proposal be modified to avoid them?
- Do other ideas share the same advantages or disadvantages, or do the advantages/disadvantages set this idea apart?

(Lumsden, Lumsden & Wiethoff, 2010).

Methods for Choosing among Alternatives

This section identifies what many people would typically call techniques of decision-making. The following tools are simply different means of narrowing, eliminating, or focusing on specific options. Because each method has its advantages and disadvantages, it is worth being thoughtful about which method to use. The group will benefit greatly from knowing the method in advance.

In a large case involving multiple firms, junior lawyers, and inexperienced lawyers, no one was in charge or asserting leadership in the brief writing process.

The younger lawyers at one firm deferred to other firms such that there ended up being dueling drafts. The end result was challenging, including multiple drafts, fundamental disagreement over the lead issue (which could have been resolved from the start), and the process was costly and inefficient due to redundancy of work, additional time spent working out the issues, and time pressure mounted. One firm finally backed off and the brief writing process moved forward.

Deference to Authority. In several situations a group or team may not make the final decision. The first scenario is where the group simply defers to the opinion of one member of the group, who may or may not be the group leader. A second scenario frequently happens where the group functions as an Advisory Committee or Task Force. Here, the group may study a problem and make recommendations, but the ultimate choice of solutions is made by an authority outside the group, such a leader or a consultant. The major advantages of these two approaches to decision making are speed, efficiency, and clarity—especially when the group is large.

These approaches to selecting among options, which rely on deferring to an internal or external expert, differ in terms of their disadvantages. A group might choose to yield its decision-making power to a member of the group because the other group members lack the confidence in their knowledge and ability. We have noticed this dynamic in law student groups, especially at the outset of working together. If one member of a student team exhibits confidence and clarity, it is easy for the others to acquiesce to the apparent expert's opinion. The problem is that, when other group members do not question or test the apparent expert's judgment, there is no guarantee that the confident student is more accurate than the others. A student who is certain about an answer can be convincingly wrong. When that is the case, the group wastes valuable time and resources before a series of poor decisions by the apparent expert prompts the group to try another approach. In our experience, student groups who initially follow this method eventually turn to other tools for choosing among the alternatives the group has developed.

Delegating decision-making to experts also occurs is where a large group, such as a nonprofit Board of Directors, delegates final authority to a sub-group of the Board, commonly called an Executive Committee. Depending on the issue, this is more efficient than attempting to resolve the issue in the large group. The Executive Committee has the benefit of the group's insights (perhaps through the nominal group technique described above), and can bring the decision to closure more quickly with fewer participants. The disadvantage of this approach is that unless there is good leadership in the Executive Committee, the decision-making process may simply start over, with the large group's input serving only as more data to weigh.

Similarly, some organizations use Advisory Committees, with the final decision being made by someone outside the group. Leaders often use an Advisory Committee or Task Force to widen the number of participants in the process. However, there are several potential pitfalls with this approach. First, a group without decision-making power may be viewed by outsiders as having no significance or power. (Rothwell, 2004). Moreover, when an Advisory Committee or Task Force has no final authority but does have an imbalance of power or status among its members, it can lead to internal factions or attempts by individuals to impress the final authority to the detriment of the group process and product. (Johnson & Johnson, 2006). For example, think of a law firm hiring committee that advises the final decision-maker—the managing partner. If the hiring committee is composed of lawyers with different status and from different practice areas within the firm the focus of some members may be on stacking the recommendations of the group to favor their practice area even if this is not in the best interest of the whole firm. Members of the hiring committee may work harder to lobby the managing partner about one candidate than to evaluate all the potential candidates for what they could contribute to the firm. Finally, the effectiveness of the Advisory Committee or Task Force model depends on the leadership skills of the person being advised, particularly that person's ability to listen, analyze, and evaluate the advice.

When a group faces time pressure, lacks confidence, or suffers internal conflict, it might shift from the best route to a decision to the easiest route. The easiest route is to abandon the group's decision-making power and leave the decision to the expert, whether inside or outside the team.

These methods abandon the value that can come from consulting the diverse perspectives and knowledge base of the team members. We encourage any group or team using this book to avoid using these methods when possible. Even if a member of the group appears to be particularly knowledgeable and confident about a particular solution, the group will likely reach a better outcome if the other group members are willing and able to challenge and question the apparent expert. Rarely does one person hold all the answers. The whole point of a team or group process is that even the best ideas can be improved if subjected to a good process. Advisory Committees or Task Forces may be necessary when wide participation is desirable, and if the group lacks decision-making power, then the group must work harder to help the ultimate authority understand the options and listen to the range of views. Moreover, the decision maker must be especially skilled in listening and analysis. Otherwise, the group process will be a waste of time.

Voting. Sometimes a group decision is just the mathematical product of many individual decisions. The strength of any voting system is that it is quick and involves all of the group members. The downside is voting may be just a decision reached through counting more than consideration.

Here's an example of voting in practice. New counsel was brought into case after the appellate court decision and before the en banc petition. There were multiple clients' (over 2 dozen) counsel and they were voting on issues related to changes in the brief. As new counsel took over they decided not to address the voting issue (but hoped that it would not reappear) and just forged forward as they deemed best. The voting issue did not recur until the very end of the brief filing process when discussing the specific relief to seek. Counsel decided to let them vote and they reached the same result counsel thought appropriate.

Ultimately a voting process will satisfy all members of group only after sufficient discussion and due consideration of all perspectives. Many formal or large group meetings are organized under Robert's Rules of Order. Robert's Rules do not permit a vote until a basic process is followed. First a motion (proposal) is made by one member of the group, and a different member of the group must "second" the motion before it can be discussed or voted upon. Next, all the members are invited to discuss the motion, one at a time, in the order recognized by the meeting leader. When the members believe the motion has been sufficiently discussed, a member can call for a vote, and if the call for a vote is seconded there can be a vote. If there is no second the discussion continues until there is agreement (through another call that is "seconded") that the group is ready for a vote.

Although parliamentary procedures such as Robert's Rules of Order may seem unnecessarily formal and arbitrary, they are intended to provide minority views with the chance to be fairly heard before they are subjected to a vote. More in-depth explanation of Robert's Rules or other parliamentary procedures falls outside the scope of this book, but any legal professional should learn the basics because when non-lawyers work with lawyers on corporate or nonprofit boards, non-lawyers frequently expect that lawyers understand parliamentary procedure. If a vote feels unfairly rushed, it can leave the losing side feeling marginalized, disgruntled, and disengaged from the decision and the organization, even though the members of the minority had a vote. In addition, when the majority fails to respect the minority's reaction, the process can create ongoing conflict and problems with implementing the group's decision.

Different voting schemes have variations of these advantages and disadvantages. We have already discussed using individual rankings or ratings as a way of organizing and analyzing team-generated ideas. One of the best uses of a voting system is to narrow and focus the discussion to only a few options that can then be more fully discussed. For example, some organizations or groups impose super-majority voting requirements to prevent the will of a simple majority from defeating the significant opposition such as where there is a 51/49 percent split. The requirement of a super-majority, such as two-thirds of the members voting, requires substantial support for a particular solution for it to be chosen as the group's decision. This requirement allows for change, although not with a significant minority. Thus, in most parliamentary procedural systems, the super-majority requirement is applied to proposals that interfere with discussion of an issue, such as a motion to limit debate or to change the agenda. (Lumsden, Lumsden & Wiethoff, 2010).

Voting is a common end-point for legal decision-making such as that of juries and the United States Supreme Court. In addition to serving as an end-point, voting is used as a preliminary means of gauging the starting positions of individual members. For example, research shows that juries frequently take straw polls early in deliberations: "between twenty to forty-five minutes" of entering the jury room for deliberations. (Devine, 2012, p. 154). As described by journalist Jeffrey Toobin, the tradition in the United States Supreme Court has been to start the Court's weekly conferences following the oral arguments cases with each member of the Court briefly describing his or her position the case, before the Court takes a vote on the outcome. (Toobin, 2007).

However, decision-making processes that ultimately resort to voting also produce frustration. American criminal law gives enormous power to even one dissenting member of a criminal jury who believes the majority is wrong, allowing that minority member to hang a jury. Lawyers and constitutional law scholars lament the uncertainty created by plurality decisions of the Supreme Court, in which five members have voted for an outcome, but no single opinion garners the agreement of five members. A plurality Supreme Court decision is an end-point for a case, but provides little guidance and much confusion on the legal issue at stake. (Stras & Spriggs, 2011). Thus, while voting can produce a result, it may not produce a satisfactory decision.

Consensus. Some researchers argue that the ideal mode of choosing among alternative solutions or options is for the team to reach consensus. (Lumsden, Lumsden and Wiefhoff, 2010). Genuine consensus among members of a group requires: agreement about a choice, a sense of satisfaction with the choice, and a commitment to that choice. (DeStephen & Hirokawa, 1988). Agreement does not mean that the solution is everyone's first choice. Consensus almost always requires compromise, settling on an acceptable choice in lieu of one's favorite. Similarly, satisfaction with the choice does not mean or require enthusiasm. Consensus does require commitment however, and with that the willingness of all members to defend and support the choice to those outside the group. Commitment separates true consensus from its evil twin, false consensus. Many people mistake a unanimous or a majority decision for consensus. However, a unanimous or majority decision can mask serious dissent and dissatisfaction that surfaces as soon as the decision is questioned by outsiders or the team tries to implement the decision.

To prevent false consensus, a team needs to build and maintain a cooperative decision-making atmosphere while encouraging dissenting views to surface and be discussed. All members must be heard. Serious concerns must be resolved to the satisfaction of those bringing them to the table or there is little hope of generating the commitment necessary to sustain the decision. For these reasons, true consensus is hard to achieve. Consensus can take much more time to achieve than other methods of choosing among alternatives, so building consensus requires patience. It also requires tolerance for conflict. As we discussed earlier, conflict can be constructive rather than destructive if parties approach it with care. Consensus requires that members treat conflicts seriously and respectfully, rather than rush to sooth and smooth over them. Thus, the more emotionally charged a decision is, the harder it will be to allow for conflict. Finally, consensus may not be possible for large groups, such as those with 15 or more members. (Rothwell, 2004).

Despite the difficulties of reaching consensus, even trying to reach consensus is beneficial. (Rothwell, 2004). The discussion required for true consensus not only produces more complete substantive analysis of the problem and alternatives, but also produces a greater sense of fairness in process. This tends to produce greater satisfaction with the team itself, even if it fails to reach consensus. Thus, groups should strive whenever possible to incorporate basic tools of reaching consensus, such as: staying focused on the problem or goal, clarifying areas of agreement, and finding ways to combine preferred alternatives if possible. (Beebe & Masterson, 2003). Even if the group has to turn to another mode of choosing in the end, such as ranked-choice voting, the overall outcome is likely to be stronger.

Implementing, Testing and Refining the Solution

Many people consider the group decision-making process finished once the group chooses its solution. However, any decision that has required the group work described so far is incomplete until it is implemented, tested, and, if necessary, refined. These finishing steps are necessary parts of the entire process. Intentionally implementing the solution, testing its effectiveness, and refining the solution are not a sign that the earlier process of generating and selecting idea was flawed. Instead, it is another part of the recursive nature of group decision-making.

A carefully designed implementation process, which incorporates time for feedback and refinement, can reduce or eliminate two common problems with group decision-making. The first problem is the error of escalation of commitment. This dynamic occurs when a group believes it has invested too much, be it time, effort, or the monetary value those factors represent, to alter or abandon its course. As a result, teams often are reluctant to revisit a decision when initial feedback reveals problems with it. Rather than revisit and reflect, the reaction can be to push harder in the same direction, hoping that the situation will improve. (Lumsden, Lumsden & Wiethoff, 2010; Brest & Hamilton Krieger, 2010).

The second problem with group decision-making is the fallout from a team's decision. When a team's decision results in significant change for an organization, the team should incorporate tactics to help the members outside the team cope with the changes. The team should also invest time to develop a strategy to implement, assess, and, if necessary, modify the decision. The decision-making process we have described so far requires thoughtfulness, which should extend all the way through the implementation stage. When a decision is sufficiently important to assign to a team, then it is also worth spending time and thought on how to best put it in practice.

To illustrate the implementation stage of decision making, including strategies for addressing resistance to change, we will use an extended example based on a recent experience one of us had as part of a faculty-generated effort to reform the first-year law school curriculum at the author's school. After several informal discussions, a handful of faculty members concluded that the first-year courses could do a much better job of:

- clarifying their objectives;
- including multiple opportunities for assessment instead of one high stakes exam at the end of the semester;
- incorporating practical, hands-on skill training in doctrinal courses;
- collaborating among courses so that students saw the need for transferring the knowledge and skills from one course to other; and
- expanding the existing first-year curriculum to include Criminal Law and Constitutional Law.

However, to make such a curriculum work, the credit hours for some courses would have to be cut substantially, which would be controversial. Despite the difficulty in implementing law school curriculum reform the team was successful in winning approval for a pilot section of the curriculum, and later, approval of full-scale implementation of the program across the first-year sections. Here's how it happened.

Analysts of effective group work frequently recommend using the Program Evaluation and Review Technique (PERT) process in the implementation stage. The Program Evaluation and Review Technique was developed by the U.S. Navy as a system for implementing complex programs, and the basic template is helpful for implementing solutions or decisions of any difficulty. The first step is to break the chosen course of action into its component steps or tasks, and assign them to group members in the sequence the tasks need to be accomplished, along with a timeline for completion. The group creates a concrete action plan which shows all the different steps, tasks, assigned group members and deadlines. The visible action plan allows the group to see its interdependence and accountability. Without this kind of planning and accountability, group work can resemble the parable reported by Professors Beebe and Masterson:

> This is a story about four people: Everybody, Somebody, Anybody, and Nobody. There was an important job to be done, and Everybody was asked to do it. Everybody was sure Somebody would do it. Anybody could have done it, but Nobody did it. Somebody got angry about that because it was Everybody's job. Everybody thought Anybody could do it, but Nobody realized that Everybody wouldn't do it. It ended up that Everybody blamed Somebody when actually Nobody asked Anybody.

(Beebe & Masterson, 2000, p. 238).

To develop the action plan, create a table with the following information:

(1) the decision, project goal, or solution to be implemented;
(2) the component actions or steps needed for completion;
(3) the sequence of the actions or the order of the component steps;
(4) an estimate of the time for each component action or step; and
(5) the name of the group member responsible for completing each step or action.

There is no one right way to organize this information so long as all the elements are included. If the solution will require resources such as money, personnel, or special supplies, the chart should also include a description of what they are, when they must be available, and who is responsible for making sure they are provided. Along with the action plan, a flow chart can be a helpful visual aid in breaking the components of the solution or action into discrete steps, putting them in the right sequence, and estimating the time required to complete them.

Figure 5.4 illustrates what an action chart might look like, while Figure 5.5 (on p. 118) shows what the related flow chart might look like, using the Pilot First-Year law school curriculum proposal as an example.

Figure 5.4 · Action Plan for Pilot First-Year Curriculum Proposal

Names							
Greg							
Ted							
Mary Pat							
Eileen							
Mehmet							
Colette							
Task	Arrange Pilot Team Meeting to Assign Tasks	Meetings with Registrar, Student Services, Vice Dean.	First Draft of Course Objectives Due to Other Pilot Team Members for Critique	Pilot Team Meeting to Discuss and Revise Course Objectives	Revised Course Objectives Posted on web site for Non-pilot Faculty to Review	Pilot Team Meets with Non-pilot Faculty to Discuss Concerns	Presentation of Proposal for Pilot First-year Section to Full Faculty
Week	1	2-3	4	1	2	3-4	2
Month	Sept.	Oct.		Nov.			December

Figure 5.5 · Flow Chart for Pilot Faculty First-Year Individual Course Curriculum Planning

When participating in the decision-making process to minimize resistance to a solution is not possible, the first task for implementation is to explain both the group's decision and the decision-making process to outsiders. (Beebe & Masterson, 2003). The team that developed the Pilot first-year curriculum tried to prepare the larger organization for the changes by having the individual Pilot Faculty members explain the Pilot objectives and how they were developed to other faculty colleagues who teach the same courses. Pilot Faculty team members met with these colleagues on an individual, face-to-face basis. Pilot Faculty used these meetings not only to educate their colleagues about why the Pilot was important, but also to learn any objections or concerns their colleagues had about the objectives or process. They could then respond to those faculty members' concerns when the Pilot was formally proposed for a vote at a meeting of the entire law school faculty.

The Pilot team was also sensitive to several other factors that help an organization accept change. First, they always tried to explain how the change mattered to the whole organization. Specifically, the Pilot team said that an integrated, sophisticated first-year curriculum that emphasized experiential learning would make the school more attractive to law school applicants in a competitive law school market. Second, to address the concerns of the other members of the law school the Pilot team stressed that the change was incremental and the burden would fall on the handful of faculty teaching it. The Pilot Faculty believed that the entire faculty, only some of whom taught first-year courses, would respond more favorably to a significant curricular change involving reduction of course credit hours if the change did not implicate their courses, at least not initially. Finally, the Pilot team emphasized that the proposed curriculum was open to revision and modification based on feedback from students, staff, and faculty both in and outside of the Pilot.

The full faculty ultimately approved the Pilot curriculum at which point the emphasis shifted from implementation to assessment. The Pilot team used many tools to assess the Pilot curriculum:

- Anonymous surveys of all students in the Pilot curriculum at several points during the academic year.
- Interviews with student government leaders about student reaction.
- Focus groups of student in the Pilot where the group leaders (two non-Pilot faculty members) could ask follow-up and clarification questions.
- Pilot Faculty self-critiques.
- Shadow critics: Pilot students who provided regular individual feedback to the coordinator, one of the creators of the Pilot who was not teaching in it. This coordinator shared feedback (anonymously) with other Pilot faculty as the courses were taught so the course could be adjusted if possible.

After a full academic year, the assessment continued into the subsequent Fall Semester. The school's faculty-student Curriculum Committee analyzed the assessment data from the previous year and gathered more of its own. Pilot students were surveyed to see how they responded to traditional courses in the second year after having had the Pilot curriculum. Faculty members who taught the Pilot were interviewed to see how they felt about returning to traditional teaching. Near the end of the semester, the Curriculum Committee ultimately recommended adopting the Pilot curriculum in all first-year sections, and the full faculty voted to do so.

This extended example of implementing a team decision was not perfect. The Pilot team did not use an action plan and flow chart as illustrated above. This led to confusion, unnecessary delays in the process, and some team members feeling excluded. Other problems surfaced, such as conflicts among Pilot team members. These kinds of conflicts, as discussed earlier in the book, arose primarily because differences in communication style and work habits were misinterpreted as personal attacks. Fortunately, the participants worked through those conflicts to forge stronger working relationships. As described here, though, the Pilot team took special care with the implementation stage,

demonstrating that thoughtful and serious attention to this stage is as important as reaching a good decision or solution.

In their book *Problem Solving, Decision Making, and Professional Judgment*,
former Stanford Law School Dean Paul Brest and Professor Linda Hamilton
Krieger describe a deliberative problem solving approach similar to Dewey's
classic Reflective Thinking model. Brest and Hamilton Krieger describe the
process as involving two styles of thinking, divergent and convergent.

> Divergent thinking expands the range of perspectives, dimensions,
> and options related to a problem. Convergent thinking eliminates pos-
> sible alternatives through the application of critical analysis, thereby
> eventually reducing the number of options that remain open. Diver-
> gent thinking conceives; convergent thinking critiques. Divergent
> thinking envisions; convergent thinking troubleshoots, fine tunes, se-
> lections and implements.

(Brest & Hamilton Krieger, 2010, p. 13). Their essential point is that a good
problem solving process requires attention to both styles of thinking.

This observation is echoed by any number of theorists who study conflict
resolution, decision-making, and problem solving. For example, some management consultants and professional development counselors use the Myers-
Briggs Type Indicator, which we discussed in Chapter Two, as a framework for
discussing decision-making. They emphasize the need to follow a "Z," or zigzag
pattern to ensure that the group brings all four mental functions into play:
Sensing, Intuiting, Thinking, and Feeling. The Sensing function emphasizes
data production, fact-finding, and problem definition while the opposite Intuiting function employs imagination to envision additional possibilities. In
making decisions, groups should ensure they zig from Sensing functions to Intuiting functions. Then, groups should zag to the Thinking function and logically analyze the effects of each possibility before zigging over to the Feeling
function to weigh the human impact of each possibility. Although everyone
uses all four mental functions at some point, some individuals gravitate more
quickly and comfortably to one of the functions. Thus, one of the benefits of
decision-making in a diverse group, is that the individual members with these
preferences, can help the group on its zigzag journey.

Whichever decision-making framework you decide to follow, take the time
to choose one. And make sure that it allows for a diversity of approaches and
talents within the group or team—balance the number crunchers with the
poets, balance the people good with quantitative data with the qualitative researchers and thinkers whenever possible. If you lack balance on a team, be
sure to seek out the missing perspectives you lack as you follow your path.

Applications

1. Describe a problem you might need to work on in a legal setting.
2. Assume that the group you are working with just jumps into working on the problem without identifying any decision-making process. Based on the materials in this text, write a script showing how one member of the group, perhaps you, could effectively engage the rest of the group in identifying and committing to a decision-making process. In the script, include group members who are reluctant to slow down and talk about the process; instead these members just want to get going.
3. Pick a topic and practice a brainstorming session with a group of students. In this simulation, assume that you have to explain and facilitate everyone's following the brainstorming guidelines. What is the hardest part of the brainstorming process for you? How might you help others overcome barriers to effective brainstorming, such as prematurely judging and critiquing ideas or being unwilling to contribute?
4. Chose a process to select among different brainstorming ideas. What are the criteria for effectiveness? How will you ensure that all voices will be heard?
5. Identify areas in the final implementation phase—how will you test for effectiveness and what language can you use to help others consider refining an adopted solution?

Chapter 6

The Logistics of Working Together

6.1 · Planning Matters

All meetings and other teamwork require planning and coordination to work well. Putting a group into action is a delicate and sophisticated task. Just because everyone is supposed to share the same work goals, does not mean they will be able to coordinate getting the work accomplished. A bit of planning and coordination in preparing, directing, and overseeing that work will go a long way to achieving success. Allowing a team to operate otherwise is akin to sending a rescue party from the mother ship with no oars, no leader, and only vague direction as to task and method. The personnel, whether carefully chosen or not, have little hope of satisfactorily accomplishing their mission.

This chapter will explore the logistics of a few areas of teamwork where planning and coordination are most needed. These areas include planning and holding group meetings, writing collaboratively, and working in virtual teams (teams that communicate primarily or exclusively through the Internet). The importance of planning was echoed in our interviews for this book by numerous clinicians, who when asked to describe successful group work, started by explaining their planning methods. For example:

> The clinician creates binders on each case so that all students can see the whole picture. Then she divides the students into teams. The teams include other lawyers and law firms, and investigators. Every team has a quarterback/leader. In advance of any group meetings, the clinician talks with the students about:

- how to give feedback;
- the importance of circulating a written agenda before meeting;
- clear communication of post-meeting assignments, including responsibilities, due dates, form of the work product, and next steps; and
- designating a meeting reporter to distribute notes to others.

This kind of planning could make the difference between a group project that results in an okay result and tepid feelings toward the experience and a great result and an eagerness to join the next group task.

6.2 · Individual Ethos, Organizational Space, and Technology

One of the authors heard the following story from several law students. It provides a good case study to analyze how some advance planning and ongoing coordination of the writing process can make a big difference in the quality of the work product and the relationships between the participants. We have broken up the case study to contrast the different approaches of the students, and the different outcomes.

> Case Study, part 1: In their first year of law school Mark and Larry self-selected as partners on a legal writing assignment. They decided to divide the writing between them, and then reconnect near the due date to exchange and compare their work. They did not discuss the assignment any further. The night before the assignment was due Mark brought a polished half of the paper and Larry showed up with an outline of his half. Mark was livid; Larry was embarrassed. They worked through the evening to finish the paper and determined never to work together again.

For several years in one of our law school's legal writing courses students worked and wrote in teams regularly. The students knew this was important to the law school because we made a big institutional push to do it. So, although Mark and Larry knew that working together was important, they did not know how to do it. In particular, students wanted to know and understand the benefits from group work. Absent clear directions students will employ trial and error, but the error rate has significant costs.

Mark disliked group work for the rest of the year, and probably beyond. Larry, the one who needed to step up, recognized that he had to approach the matter differently the next time. The professor also realized that a fairly detailed training session was needed to convey to students why they should seriously engage in their group work.

> Case Study, part 2: Larry and Julie partnered on the next group assignment. Both had had bad experiences with their previous partners. Given these experiences, both Larry and Julie were determined to learn how the other worked. That conversation revealed their respective strengths and weaknesses, and allowed them to see and appreciate what they could learn from each other. Julie was the better writer, Larry was much more detail-oriented and a clear procrastinator. They set a plan for the assignment, and divvied their responsibilities based on individual strengths, rather than individually researching and writing in parallel.

Larry and Julie understood the law school and professor's ethos on group work. They then took the time to figure out how they could work together better. This involved a great deal of reflection, setting aside pride, changing methods, and experimentation. All of these are critical to allowing good, creative solutions to appear when brainstorming of solutions to a problem.

All organizations, whether law school classrooms or clinics, public interest offices, or big law firms, need to be mindful that they are explicit about their group ethos, and careful not to send mixed messages on how to work. For example, offices where employees are physically separated from one another in cubicles, or those that provide little or no conference space conducive to group meetings, are sending a message that solitary work is more important than group work. The office with neutral physical spaces that support combining efforts, team meetings, and virtual connections between team members will find the employees more ready, willing, and able to work in groups.

In fact, once students embrace the ethos and dive into the work, they will demand or create an environment consistent with their needs.

> Case Study, part 3: The day before their brief was due, Larry and Julie were in the library. Their professor came upon them as he was walking down the library stairs. On a long set of waist-high bookcases, Larry and Julie had laid out every page of their brief in order. They were walking forward and backward amongst the pages, which enabled them to review the brief in a non-linear fashion. Periodically, they stopped, consulted, and made notations.

Julie and Larry could have simply decided to print and review the brief individually, or even together. We would argue, however, that in their case they made the physical space they needed to yield a most creative editing process and one that might not have happened otherwise.

Walking among the pages and consulting each other probably took more time than individual review. But, as argued earlier and well supported in the literature, this additional "cost" (when reducing attorney hours to billable time) resulted in an improved final product, with greater depth and breadth.

> Case Study, part 4: After watching Larry and Julie for several minutes, the professor approached and asked them what they were doing. They responded that after having worked closely together on paper and electronically, they needed to be able to look at their work in a different way. So they laid out every page to enable them to read it forward, backward, and any way in between. They could also then better visualize how the smaller pieces made up the whole brief.
>
> Case Study, part 5: Later Larry and Julie approached the professor and asked to be considered as co-Teaching Assistants for legal writing the following year. The professor hired them on the spot.

Educating people about teamwork never stops. As new personnel bring in new baselines and continuing people revert to old habits, there is great need to repeatedly communicate the benefits and process of group work, offer training sessions, and have employees share experiences. It is important that students and attorneys receive a consistent and consistently positive message regarding teamwork.

Just as the professor hired Julie and Larry, a legal organization must also show that it values an individual's contribution to group work.

> Case Study, aftermath: Larry now works in a very large corporate law firm. Early on in his practice in preparation for an international arbitration he had to submit his client's evidence for the hearing. Rather than just giving Larry the task and reviewing it upon completion, the Senior Associate sat with him and walked through all of the documents, explaining the case, the issues, the relevance or lack thereof of the documents, and they put together the appropriate collection of evidentiary materials. This took 6 hours, but by the end both were confident that Larry could manage the task individually the next time.

Ignoring this key point could undermine the most well thought out physical structure, employee training program, and management buy-in for sustained teamwork. If individual work is still the ultimate mark for grades, promotion, or advancement, then the students and attorneys will revert to an individualistic approach to work even if that sacrifices the client's best interests. Precisely how to strike this balance will vary from setting to setting.

6.3 · Effective Group Meetings

Once the law office or other legal organization shows it values group work in its physical space, ethos, and training, how can individuals make sure that their group meetings work as well as possible? How do you set up a meeting so that attendance, participation, and follow through are not only critical to personal responsibility, but also to the greater good of the organization? How many times have you attended a meeting where one or more of the following questions went unanswered?

- "Who needs to attend?"
- "What are we talking about?"
- "How long will this take?"
- "What's the follow up?"

And if the meeting organizer is someone higher up the hierarchy than those called to the meeting, who wants to tell the "boss" that she blew it by not asking "Henry" to attend? Likewise, who wants to add more work to their already overflowing plate of work? How many meetings could be saved if someone asked, "Why do we need a meeting? What is the goal?" As one attorney observed, "It really helps being more intentional about the goal of the meeting.... Sometimes the goal is just for sharing information and engaging the group.... [It's] frustrating when people attending a meeting are thinking, why am I here?" This lawyer also noted the importance of having all attending a meeting prepare for the meeting and be engaged in it. "There are problems when people go to a meeting with the wrong expectations because they didn't listen earlier or didn't recognize that the focus shifted in the meeting." If you listen to this lawyer carefully you will hear frustrations on two different levels, a task level and a relationship level. Effective collaborative work in meetings requires awareness and attention to both of these dimensions of teamwork.

6.3.1 · Navigating the Task Dimension

A good starting place to address the task dimension of group work is to establish some ground rules, explicit statements agreed upon by all members of the group about how the group will operate. Ground rules are different from team "norms," which are standards or habits that can develop even unconsciously. When we describe typical group behavior, we are talking about the group norms. Teams will inevitably develop norms, but teams have to consciously create ground rules. For example, a norm might be that the group engages in 5 minutes of social talk before starting the discussion of the work for that meeting. A ground rule is a written or oral commitment of all members to begin the meeting exactly on time. Research suggests that teams are more efficient if they develop explicit ground rules. Anyone on a group or team can suggest the creation of ground rules. Simply ask for them, saying, "What would the rest of you think if we established some ground rules for our meetings?" Examples of typical ground rules are:

- Every meeting will begin on time.
- Each team member will be prepared for each meeting.
- We will listen carefully to the points being made.
- We will turn our smartphones off and put them out of reach unless we need to use them for team purposes, such as setting the date of the next meeting.
- We will make decisions by consensus rather than by majority vote.
- We agree to stick to the agenda, making notes of topics that come up that are outside the agenda for discussion at the end of the meeting or at the next meeting.
- We will run our meetings by Robert's Rules of Order.
- We will hold each other accountable for following these ground rules.

When there are clear ground rules, team members have an objective basis for discussing problems with the performance of a team member. For example, if the frustrated lawyer we discussed above had specific ground rules to point to, she could say to her group, "Hey, I know that it feels as if there is more work than we can handle right now, but I am worried that we are drifting away from the assignment we gave ourselves for this meeting. Since we all agreed to listen carefully and stick to the agenda, we need to get back to our focus." The lawyer does not have to be a scold. She is just doing what all of the team members agreed to do, hold each other accountable to the ground rules.

Another important part of ensuring the success of the task level of team meetings is to prepare and distribute a meeting agenda. An agenda is simply a plan for structuring the group discussion. We have seen far too many groups struggle because they lacked an agenda. Even the most short-term group can use an agenda. For example, suppose a Contracts professor assigns a short group work project:

In your assigned groups, please read the four possible examples of an indemnification clause I have given you, discuss them together, and choose the best version to include in our class's sample contract between Acme and XYZ companies. You have 20 minutes to do this task, then I will call on groups to discuss their choice with the class.

We know how many student groups would approach this. They just start reading the examples, without creating an agenda. This means that the fastest readers finish reviewing the examples and want to start discussing the options, or just start talking about which example they prefer while the other members of the group are still reading and thinking. Recall the discussion in Chapter Two about communication preferences and styles. Some group members (extroverts) need to "think out loud," while other group members (introverts) need quiet time to think before they speak. This group invariably concludes it does not have enough time to do the task assigned. A group in this situation is going to be more effective if, before starting to work on task, the group takes less than a minute to sketch out an agenda. One group member might say:

> OK, let's take three minutes to read through these to ourselves, and another two minutes to individually and silently rank our preferred clauses and think about why we think they are the best. Then we can have ten minutes to go around the group and explain our choices. Then we have five minutes to finalize our decision.

In our experience, this group will not run out of time, will spot more of the advantages and disadvantages in the group's options, and will come up with good reasoning for their final choice. Plus, the introverts get time to think and the extroverts get time to talk, making them more satisfied and comfortable with the group process.

Who should create the agenda? It can be spontaneous as described above, or in some cases, the authority calling the group together will appoint the leader, for example, designating a committee chair. It can help to have a designated leader especially if:

- the team is large;
- the team has not worked together before;
- the task is highly complex;
- obvious interpersonal conflicts in the team need to be carefully managed; or
- a single voice is needed immediately for clear communications between the team and the larger organization.

(Lumsden, Lumsden & Wiethoff, 2010). A designated leader might have the clearest picture of the work direction, can give notice of what needs to be covered, and assign roles to team members, increasing the efficiency of the group.

Even where there is a designated leader, we have stressed throughout this book that every member of a team or group has responsibility for leading it to success. We have emphasized that you do not need to be "in charge" to be a good group leader. Some teams or groups may even choose to operate without a designated leader, choosing to be self-managed. That means the group members might share the work of being the primary leader. For instance, team members might rotate the task of preparing for and leading meetings according to a schedule. This way, no one person gets stuck with all of the organization work. Other teams may rotate management responsibility so they can take some time to determine which members have particularly important skills, such as organizational skills or interpersonal skills, before they choose a particular person to be the leader. In some self-managed teams, leaders may emerge as their unique abilities become clear to the members of the team and can be matched to the task at hand. (Wolff, Pescosolido & Druskat, 2002). Leaders who emerge from the group derive power not from the outside, but from within the team, which can be a tremendous asset.

Regardless of whether a leader is designated or emerges from the group, it is important to have someone manage team meetings. To prepare the agenda, the meeting leader can invite, collect, and assess suggestions from the members for issues or topics to be discussed. Someone other than the leader should be assigned or volunteer to take notes of the meeting, focusing on listing the follow-up tasks, individuals assigned, and deadlines for work discussed at the meeting. A well thought out agenda distributed in advance, coupled with detailed post-meeting notes with specific post-meeting assignments, deadlines, and reporting obligations will ensure that everyone on the team will have a sufficient amount of certitude about what they are doing, how to do it, and when it needs to be done.

6.3.2 · Navigating the Relationship Dimension

To this point we have focused on the task dimension of leading meetings. In addition, the person who manages a meeting must be sensitive to the relationship dimension. One of the attorneys we spoke to worked with a variety of constituents on international environmental law issues and discussed the importance of leading effective meetings.

> There is a set of skills we [lawyers] look down on, like running a meeting. We are not taught to value the skills of organizing, building a

coalition, and facilitating a discussion. We underestimate the importance of political influence. We think that as lawyers, we can say something should get done and it will be done. If we are smart, people should listen to us. We don't recognize that maybe our approach as lawyers, focusing on confrontation and litigation, is not helpful. There are some skills we are good at, like word-smithing, but when you are working with groups you have to be aware of the dynamics of meetings. Putting the organization first. Letting go of ego. Getting everybody on the same page to get to a unified outcome. A lot of lawyers tend to dominate the discussions. They trump any other voice in the room. They stifle the conversation. They make the discussion all about legal issues. It's important that legal voices don't shape the entire direction of the meeting. Attorneys should see themselves not always as leaders but as the legal technicians. They need to listen to the issues and consider what is best.

This lawyer is absolutely right—leading meetings does not mean dominating meetings. One of us once served on a committee in which the Chair sat the head of the conference table, with the other committee members on each side of him. Every time a member of the committee spoke, the Chair would comment or respond to that individual before allowing other members to speak. The meetings became a series of dialogues between the Chair and Member X, the Chair and Member Y, the Chair and Member Z, and so on. These committee meetings were painful experiences, and the work of the committee took far more time than necessary.

The leader of a meeting should speak up, however, when a member has been particularly harsh or strident stating her position. This is the moment to use the wisdom of the group. The chair can use the opportunity to seek the views of other members of the group. As law firm management consultant Gerald Riskin explains, someone at the meeting might say:

> "I think it's inappropriate to open a branch office in [so-and-so]," or "I do not think we should move forward with this plan for attracting clients." ...
>
> Instead of reacting, instead of debating, effective leaders turn to the group and say, "Are there any other thoughts on that?"
>
> Almost without fail, someone in the rest of the group will balance the argument.... This phenomenon is so reliable that it is almost amazing to watch. Like air filling a vacuum in physics, someone will come along to balance the argument.

(Riskin, 2005, p. 137). Then, the leader can take the various positions described, summarize them, and invite efforts to reconcile the concerns in light of the group's goals.

Leading meetings and conflict management will converge at times. We addressed general methods for conflict management in Chapter Four. Here's an example that relates to both in the context of a meeting. A junior partner at a mid-size specialized firm offered us these additional tips for managing effective meetings: "Be respectful about time. People appreciate it when the leader of a meeting runs a tight ship. You have to shut people down when they start to pontificate. You have to end on time." When people start to go off on tangents or belabor a point, this partner is not bashful about interrupting them, "Well, we have a big agenda, so let's move on." He adds, "I also hold up my hands. I learned this from someone else. I use it all the time. It really works in getting people to stop talking. Attorneys love to get on their soap boxes. Another technique I'll use is I'll poll the group: 'I'd like to poll the group. I'd like everyone to raise their hands if they think we should continue.'" Often the person talking, the partner pointed out, doesn't realize that everyone else is ready to move on. Another approach he uses is to play devil's advocate or identify someone else who will likely have a different view. "'Hold on, I'd like to hear from....' That way the group can get the other side, which often allows the group to transition to another topic." As these suggestions illustrate, to get the most productive contributions from members at the meeting, the meeting leader should try to keep her opinions, or the opinions of any particular member, from dominating the discussion. As we have stressed throughout the book, especially in discussing decision making, a team needs to have the information and diverse insight of all of its members to produce the best outcomes. This will not happen if one or more members dominate the discussions.

6.3.3 · Bringing Task and Relationship Together

When the team's work is ongoing, the team must pay special attention to the task and the relationship dimensions. Thus, the first team meeting is a critical opportunity to build rapport and trust, define the purpose and goals of the group, establish the short-term and long-term expectations, assign roles, share the method(s) for evaluation, and set the tone for all work to be done by the team. Either the person(s) who created the team or the team leader needs to raise, explain, and answer questions about each of these from the start.

Because many lawyers and law students are unenthusiastic about teamwork and often quite skeptical, during the first meeting, the team leader should engage the team members in discussing the following questions:

- What are the concerns of team members?
- How will their work be monitored?
- What should they do if someone is slacking?
- How do they handle disagreement and conflict?
- What are the expected or preferred means of communication?

Engaging everyone in discussing these questions is particularly important because natural skepticism of teamwork can run deep. In addition, law students' high degree of skepticism of group work can manifest as students having much stronger negative than positive expectations about group work. (Narko, Inglehart & Zimmerman, 2003). And while those preconceptions cannot be swayed through directions, they can be changed in a very real way through well designed and implemented teamwork.

Finally, a group needs to have a common understanding of its goals, and address any fear of individual or group failure. Team members must address goals and potential failures in the first meeting. Larry and Mark never gave themselves a chance to discuss these before the fear of failure took over as the only driving force to complete the task and terminate the team. Julie and Larry recognized this and took many steps to ensure that they shared their goals and methods. Trust grew through their work, led to effective communication, helped them be creative, and enabled them to deliver a great final product.

Although the task and relationship dimensions of meetings are equally important to effective collaborative work, sometimes the relationship dimensions outlast the significance of the particular task. A lawyer working for a large government agency recently illustrated her new appreciation for the value of meetings. "I used to dread going to meetings. I couldn't see the value of just sitting and listening to people drone on." She quickly realized that meetings were valuable opportunities to develop and build relationships. "Now I sit in every staff meeting and take notes. If there is anything interesting I follow up. I'll introduce myself, tell them what my office does, and see if there is anything we can help them with." After two months of meetings, offering to help, and asking more questions, this lawyer had tripled the number of people she was friendly with in a major department, allowing her to be a much more effective contributor to her own department. She had this advice for law students: "Always carry a pen and paper." She had been at a meeting where a superior was complaining about a problem. The lawyer picked up her pen and started writing, offering to see if she could take care of the problem. The supervisor said, "That's the first time in years someone has said 'I'll take care of it' and started writing." The relationship skills this junior partner developed doing teamwork have made her a far more valuable member of her firm.

6.4 · Writing in Teams

There is no basis to think that writing cannot be shared among individuals. The initial urge when a team reaches the writing stage is to divide and conquer. This divide and conquer process means that teammates cut the task into discrete parts, assign each part to one person, then have one person pull the pieces together, edit out style differences, and insert transitions. While the divide and conquer process certainly will result in a written work that is a team product, it should not be the default method and groups should recognize that it might not necessarily result in the best final product.

Julie and Larry, and many other student pairs, sat together at the same computer monitor, forming sentence after sentence and paragraph after paragraph. Why go through all this time and effort? The product of such a joint venture will be powerful and not need nearly as much stylistic editing as the divide and conquer method. One of the authors has been witness to this process with first, second, and third year law students. While the shared writing process is time consuming, the final product is usually one of, if not the, best produced in the class.

When does the divide and conquer process make more sense? If the issues are discrete, then division is not only sensible, but also the argument might benefit from a variation in writing styles to differentiate the points. Either way, the decision on the writing process should be thoughtful, and not default.

On the continuum between divide and conquer and close collaboration there are many variations that may be best in light of the assignment, the information to be reported, or the group dynamics. One variation is where the team brainstorms the topics to be included, the order of presentation, and any specific stylistic concerns. The team selects one person to write the first draft, and then everyone participates in editing the draft. The final product of this effort will reflect everyone's contributions and also avoids editing for writing style. This process might be best when several different attorneys representing different clients want to file a single brief. This can happen where many of the issues are the same, thus it is efficient for all parties, but they all want a brief that does not read as if each part had a different author. Other variations are as limitless as the group's imagination, but the central point is to take the time to talk through and decide on the writing and editing process.

In deciding on a writing process, lawyers must be mindful that movement toward divide and conquer brings with it more individualistic focus in the writing and in the product, while movement toward pure joint writing increases the integrated nature of the writing. The latter will necessitate more time at the beginning of the writing process, while the former will require more at the end. And sometimes, time will dictate the process when there just is not enough time to discuss words, phrases, sentences, and the like.

Finally, regardless of the process, the writers' task is challenging in many ways. The writers are charged with reflecting everyone's input, the best points, and filtering out unnecessary points, essentially boiling down the group's work to present it as clearly as possible. The onus is on the writers to both aggregate the necessary information and to weave together any different voices.

A senior associate in a large multinational firm illustrated some of the challenges of group writing, telling us, "[It's ineffective when] people don't effectively prioritize. Not everything in a document is at the same level of importance. When you are down to the wire, making suggestions about the format is better left unsaid. Don't inject stupid ideas—prioritize. You just have to let some stuff go." He noted that at his current firm, a number of writing teams had no effective method of collaborating. In contrast, as his former large firm, "there was always one document that everyone worked on and only one person 'had the pen' and was able to make final decisions and edits. There was ... one person [assigned] to put together all the final versions. Also, attorneys always announced by email when they were 'in the document' so everyone knew." Having this kind of structured process reduces stress and frustration and results in more effective documents.

Another lawyer working for a governmental agency described to us the problems that arose when teams didn't collaborate effectively to produce document. "Last summer, many people had to sign off on a report. It was a perfect storm. Lots of people were on vacation and we were stuck with a deadline. It was a mess. No one knew who was in charge. Getting the information was like pulling teeth." Now when this lawyer works on a writing project, she builds in extra time so that she can take the time to meet with people, talk about the project, and work on it with people in person. "I have internal deadlines. I give them forewarning, like telling [them] that a court monitor will ... want a report ... and will be coming in June. I'll ask for the information I need two to four weeks before the real deadline, depending on the person. I recognize when I have downtimes and will help people when I have time."

6.5 · The Special Challenges of Virtual Teams

Virtual teams are neither new nor particularly innovative. Rather they are now more of a necessity with the available technology, a rising generation who have been communicating virtually for most of their lives, and law offices teaming with individuals in all corners of the globe. On the practical side, when the right people for a team are in different places, it will always be less expensive to meet virtually than fly everyone to a meeting. Face-to-face interactions with all team members in one location are likely to continue to decline as everyone grows more comfortable with technology and communicates more readily in virtual settings like email, social networking venues, and instant communication feeds like Twitter and RSS. At work we share network drives and share documents through web resources like Google docs, Netdocuments, Dropbox, and Sharepoint. We mark up electronic documents using word processing programs, build virtual databases and information compilations like wikis, and carry out lengthy conversations on blogs. The speed and breadth of these changes is best marked by the discourse around disappearing cultural information sources, such as landline telephones and paper-based news sources, such as daily newspapers and weekly magazines. (Thomson, 2009).

Video conferences, video depositions, distance education, webinars, and the plethora of on-line video communication (beyond the availability of your favorite network shows and movies) illustrate the ease of virtual connections. These connections mimic live encounters and ultimately facilitate team functionality where team members are not geographically close enough to communicate face-to-face on a regular basis. As a result, some law firms are going completely "virtual," with no shred of permanent physical office presence. (Burton, 2013).

This technology gets better and cheaper every day, and team connections ensure that work is done, done properly, and does not sacrifice quality. Some believe there is no substitute for meeting in person, for seeing live an individual's non-verbal responses, for hearing firsthand the tone and inflection of a person's voice, and the like. While that view may require having some face-to-face gatherings as well as the best technology, that traditional view cannot persist without some adaptation to modern realities. Thus, as we discuss below, it is more helpful to focus on the specific challenges of virtual teams and be thoughtful and intentional in addressing those challenges directly.

6.5.1 · A Closer Look at Virtual Team Challenges

Virtual teams face the same challenges as other teams and then some. Several matters unique to virtual realities bear discussion before a close examination of several particularly challenging ones. First, distractions or competing demands for attention affect the virtually connected, including the challenges between prioritizing virtual teamwork and non-virtual assignments. When these compete, non-virtual assignments usually win out. In addition, virtual teams face distractions that arise once focused on the virtual teamwork. The latter includes both matters in the present world, such as people, other files, phone calls, etc., and virtual distractions such as email, surfing the internet, Facebook, games, etc.

Second, ambiguity that abounds in all communication is compounded when communication is virtual. Misread emails can lead to vast gulfs in relationships, as well as to the misunderstanding of work and assignments. Even if perfect from the drafter's perspective, an email's language, tone, and room for inferences all make the message susceptible to being misread by the recipient without the drafter being able to correct or clarify until and unless the recipient engages the author.

In any meeting, ambiguity in communication during a meeting can also arise when one or more people dominate the conversation and others do not speak. This is a challenge of facilitation and enforcing ground rules. But the lack of contribution and the inability to understand the inequality of contribution can be more difficult to see and address in a virtual meeting, and can lead to many assumptions, like "John is not interested in this project," or "Sarah is a real go-getter and should be assigned more important tasks." These assumptions are not necessarily supported by the facts. (Crampton, 2001).

Third, building rapport and trust in relationships takes time, effort, and interaction. In a virtual setting, these are not part of the interaction like in face-to-face interactions. People feel less comfortable with and confident in trusting individuals who are not present. As a result, in a virtual setting we start from a position of distrust and require proof of worthiness before reaching comfortable levels in the relationship. (Lin, Standing & Liu, 2008).

Fourth, lawyers on virtual teams must be especially sensitive to their professional ethical responsibilities of confidentiality. (Burton, 2013; Kennedy & Mighell, 2008). We are all aware of the pitfalls of accidental disclosure or forwarding information to opposing counsel because of hitting the "send" button too soon, but there are many more potential problems lurking when we communicate with clients or other teams of lawyers or store documents in the cloud or on servers over which we may not have control. This topic is beyond the scope of this book, but every lawyer has a responsibility to ensure the security of her confidential communications, whether they are face-to-face or virtual.

Finally, if the technology is difficult to use or does not work well due to speed, access, or quality, participants have an incentive not to engage. Virtual team members may become quickly focused on finding another matter to work on or be frustrated by the project. One author was just on a conference call when suddenly everyone's words echoed repeatedly. Everyone hung up and redialed the conference number, but the echo continued. The author then hung up, turned attention to other tasks, and periodically checked email for an update. Virtual meetings may also project technology frustrations onto all virtual tasks or all teamwork. This decreases the effectiveness of a virtual team, and may lead to other problems.

6.5.2 · Starting Right: Build Trust and Rapport

The way to build and ensure trust relationships among virtual team members lies in the team planning. Trust is built among team members through interaction in comfortable ways, which includes early face-to-face gathering, setting clear ground rules and norms for teamwork, structuring the work to necessitate positive interaction, and rewarding trust and relationships.

There is no perfect replacement for human interaction, so incorporating some face-to-face interaction at some point, preferably early on, is highly useful with virtual teams. (Burton, 2013; Maznevski & Chudoba, 2000). If not possible, then the team builder should consider choosing team members who have had past face-to-face contact. (Pauleen 2003; Lin, Standing & Liu, 2008). For long-term projects, periodic face-to-face meetings have been shown to establish, confirm, and grow trust. (Saunders, 2000).

In the first team gatherings, whether virtual or face-to-face, the group has to set ground rules and norms for conduct, interaction, work product, and the like. These standards must be explicit, discussed, and reached by consensus. (Sarker, Lau, & Sahay, 2001). Because virtual media are impersonal and challenging for some to conceptualize, it should be clear that communications and interactions in virtual settings will be treated the same as face-to-face interactions with trust, respect, and an openness that welcomes and values all contributions. The message should be that "we value information and perspectives equally and often." While this should go without saying, make no such assumption in the virtual world. When the medium is different, behavior changes. Everyone on the team must be instructed to proceed on the presumption of trust unless and until behavior raises a concern, and any such concern must be brought to the team leader or a specified individual. (Meyerson, Weick, & Kramer, 1996; Kruempel, 2000).

Teambuilding exercises can be done with virtual team members. (Kaiser, Tullar, & McKowen, 2000). With technology such as instant messaging programs or texting, which allow for side conversations or one-to-one conversations with the moderator, virtual teams can use traditional group ice-breakers, such as talk with another group member, and then introduce that person to the rest of the group. Further, teambuilding can be built into or out of the structure of the work and the work assignments. For example, assume that a group of lawyers working on a criminal appeal have identified 13 errors in the record and each error has a separate constitutional or procedural basis. If most team members canvassed a limited part of the record for appealable issues, even if the team discussed the potential issues and agreed on the issues to be raised on appeal, the team leader could maintain discrete work by assigning each issue to the individual who read that section of the record. Without any encouragement, team members will operate as lone rangers or as a wagon wheel where the spokes connect to the hub or on the periphery, but not to each other.

Alternatively, the lead attorney could force team members to build relationships and share information by simply having everyone read overlapping portions of the record and mixing the assignments so that the attorneys research and write on an issue in a different section of the record than they read. While this may appear inefficient because multiple people are reading the same section of the record, this extra work will create common avenues to discuss issues. Furthermore, the cross-pollination of ideas that came with the initial issue sharing will continue and create an obvious person to call with questions and to test ideas. This creation of teams within the team should also give everyone a better sense of the bigger picture of the case, make the pieces created fit together better, and require less editing in the end.

6.5.3 · Starting Strong: Making Technology Work for You

Technology must facilitate virtual teamwork through training on using the technology and having a support system to address and correct issues that arise. (Sarker & Sahay, 2002). Many software or hardware packages have additional components to facilitate and support virtual teamwork. Some use may raise broader concerns regarding its use, flexibility, and limitations, such as the use of off-site information storage, like a private server and concerns about confidential information, work-product, and privilege.

When word processing software first came into use, many older attorneys who could not type continued to handwrite and give that work to an assistant to type. Not only did this refusal to engage the technology limit the attorney's ability to create work product (to the extent word processing can improve the product), but it also created a gulf between the attorney work and technology that only grew larger as technology expanded. Regular use of technology will bring comfort, and reveal any weaknesses in the user or the software. Once these weaknesses are identified, they can be addressed.

Law students and lawyers will quickly become frustrated with technology if glitches occur frequently, are difficult to address, have unforeseen effects such as slowing down other computer functionality, or support is unavailable during the hours of use. One author has held numerous virtual meetings well past the end of the normal workday. He always started the process by working with IT to ensure that support would be there from start to finish. He also has experienced the dark side of technology. On a recent call-in seminar with 50–75 people, many things failed to go well. First there was no circulated agenda, and when one document was circulated some people still did not receive it. Then someone put the call on hold forcing the speaker to talk over the hold music. When someone asked for an example or exercise and the speaker suggested one, many people made counter-suggestions. Nor did the recommenders back down when the speaker tried to explain why those suggestions would not work. That is when, as mentioned above, everyone's words started to echo. Seemingly all of this could have been avoided with a bit of planning and more adept use of technology.

6.5.4 · Managing Culture and Communication Issues on Virtual Teams

To achieve common understanding among virtual team members some time should be spent looking for any cultural differences that could lead to ambiguity. (Burton, 2013; Zolin, Hinds, Fruchter & Levitt, 2004). Many teams are virtual because certain levels of expertise could only be found at great distance. Here, it is even more important to ensure that everyone understands the language and terms. To prevent misunderstanding and confusion, many teams will define terms, build glossaries, and actively identify variant language even before requests for clarity. Further, documents posted for editing and comment should encourage requests for clarification. In the law, eliminating ambiguity is a perennial concern and preoccupation, and must be given special attention when dealing with foreign languages or specialized terms. (Majchrzak, Rice, King, Malhotra & Ba, 2000; Suchan & Hayzak, 2001).

Team communications, whether at a meeting or in other interactions, should be facilitated or self-facilitated. Whoever is vested with this responsibility needs to more actively undertake the task in a virtual setting where distractions are readily at hand and where you cannot see if the person is on or off task. As an extreme example, if someone falls asleep during a face-to-face meeting, someone else will notice and hopefully act to bring the member who nodded off back into the conversation. However, in a virtual meeting, if someone falls asleep no one might notice until that person failed to disconnect at the end of the meeting. Thus, the virtual facilitator is obligated to nudge, prod, or otherwise engage everyone during the meeting to ensure not only that she is not asleep, but also that she feels included, that there is space for her contributions, and that her views are considered in the mix of conversation. Whoever facilitates will need instruction on what is expected of them in that role. For teams expected to self-facilitate, everyone must be trained on these techniques. Whether motivated by concern over slacking or distractions, supervisors of virtual teams and off-site work need to establish express norms and practices to ensure that work is done and done as expected. (Sarker, Lau & Sahay, 2001). On the one hand, a supervisor could use software that allows one to view another person's screen and limit access to certain sources, such as the Internet. This method, while quite effective, sends a clear message that the supervisor distrusts those she works with. At the other extreme, a supervisor could not care about distractions, such as hours of web surfing, so long as the work is done by the deadline. This defers all decision-making and prioritization of work to the team member. A middle position involves periodic check-ins, such as the ability to view another's workstation, live or via stored information, and scheduled progress updates with drafts of the work product.

Where one falls on this oversight continuum depends, ultimately, on how the team was chosen, trained, instructed, and motivated, and what expectations were established. Picking the right people for the task, assigning a strong leader, and setting the right tone for the work will go a long way to avoiding these issues. Like any other adventure, virtual teamwork will translate into a positive and powerful experience if it is engaged in a way to maximize its potential.

Applications

Group writing: In groups of three or four, try out the two extremes of group writing through two exercises. As a group, you will write two brief articles using two different methods.

1. First, choose a scribe and write collectively as a group, everyone working together at the same time. Write a half-page article explaining how to gain admission to law school. Take care to make the article as well-crafted as possible, as though it were to be submitted to the magazine editor when you are finished.
2. Next, write another article, this one two pages long, explaining how to succeed in law school. This time, break up the paper and assign each person a section to write, and then come together to put them together.
3. Consider the two approaches.

   • Which method do you prefer?

- How does the quality of the two articles compare?
- Did one method take significantly more time than the other?
- Would a hybrid be more effective? What would that look like?

Virtual meetings: Next time you are on the telephone at work, consciously think about what else draws your attention.

- Do you peek at email? Do you check your calendar? Do you surf the web? Which, if any, of these tasks related to the call?
- If you ever try to read something while someone else is talking, what do you remember from what was said and what you read?
- How do you feel when you speak on the phone and the response indicates that the person was not paying attention to what you said?

Chapter 7

Working Together,
Now and Beyond

The old adage "nothing good comes easy" readily applies to group work. As we describe in the preceding chapters, your ability to reflect on your strengths and weaknesses, to focus on and adjust certain skills, and to engage others are essential to your success, and will certainly present challenges. We hope you have seen that within each chapter of the book, we tried to pay attention to both the big picture and the nuts and bolts of working well together. Moreover, each chapter has tried to address the two overall dimensions of collaborative work: tasks and relationships.

Effective law offices and teams value individuals who are good at both the detail work and the big picture. Thus, we have shared the experiences of law students and lawyers who understand that the practice of law involves attention to relationships as much as skillful legal analysis. Working effectively in groups and teams requires vigilant attention to these multiple dimensions, back and forth, zooming out and zooming in. No wonder it is so difficult at times.

Use the resources referenced for further understanding of the topics covered. Do not hesitate to pursue greater depths of understanding. If one collaborative experience is ineffective, use it as a learning opportunity for the next time. Avoid the trap of "I tried it once and it didn't work." We believe everyone can work with others more effectively and with greater satisfaction. So we encourage you to use, reuse, and share this book as you work on teams. We are confident that you will be pleased with the growth and development you experience along the way.

Help Us to Continue the Dialogue

As we conclude this book, we hope that it is a catalyst for legal professionals, including law students, to have more conversations and learn more about effective group work. We are eager to learn more about your experiences with collaborative work. In this vein, we invite you to share your stories about legal team, group, or collaborative work—whatever you call it—so that we can include the lessons from those experiences in subsequent editions of this book. In other words, we hope to keep working together, with our readers, to help legal professionals work well together! Our email addresses are:

scallen@law.ucla.edu
Sophie.Sparrow@law.unh.edu
c-zimmerman@law.northwestern.edu

Thank you.

References

Abrams, L. (2006). Using type to help lawyers find career satisfaction. *APT Bulletin of Psychological Type.* 29(2): 8–10.

American Bar Ass'n, Section of Legal Educ. & Admissions to the Bar. (1992). Legal education and professional development—an educational continuum: Report of the Task Force on law schools and the profession: Narrowing the gap. ["The MacCrate Report"].

Beckman, L.J. (1970). Effects of students' performance on teachers' and observers' attributions of causality. *Journal of Educational Psychology.* 61:76–82.

Beebe, S.A. & Masterson, J.T. (2003). *Communicating in small groups: Principles and practices* (7th ed.). Boston, MA: Allyn & Bacon.

Beebe, S.A. & Masterson, J.T. (2000). *Communicating in small groups: Principles and practices* (6th ed.). New York: Longman.

Beebe, S.A. & Mottet, T.P. (2010). *Business and professional communication: Principles and skills for leadership.* Boston, MA: Allyn & Bacon.

Blake, R.R. & Mouton, J.S. (1964). *The managerial grid.* Houston: Gulf Publishing.

Bormann, Ernest G. (1975). *Discussion and group methods.* New York: Harper & Row.

Brest, P. & Hamilton Krieger, L. (2010). *Problem solving, decision making, and professional judgment: a guide for lawyers and policy makers.* Cambridge, MA: Oxford University Press.

Brown, V. & Paulus, P.B (1996). A simple dynamic model of social factors in group brainstorming. *Small Group Research.* 27: 91–114.

Burton, C. (2013). Managing a virtual law firm. *Law Practice.* 39(2): March/April. Retrieved May 2, 2013, from http://www.americanbar.org/publications/law_practice_magazine/2013/march-april/managing-a-virtual-law-firm.html.

Cain, S. (2012). *Quiet: The power of introverts in a world that can't stop talking*. New York: Crown Publishers.

Carpenter, D. (2012). *Flagrant conduct: The story of Lawrence v. Texas: How a bedroom arrest decriminalized gay Americans*. New York: W. W. Norton & Co.

Cassidy, R.M. (2012). Beyond practical skills: Nine steps for improving legal education now. *Boston College L. Rev.* 53: 1515–1531.

Cialdini, R.B. (2006). *Influence: The psychology of persuasion* (revised ed.). New York: William and Morrow.

Cooke, R.A. & Kernaghan, J.A. (1987). Estimating the difference between group versus individual performance on problem-solving tasks. *Group & Organizational Studies.* 12(3): 319–342.

Cragan, J.F., Wright, D.W. & Kasch, C.R. (2004). *Communication in small groups: Theory, process, skills* (6th ed). Belmont, CA: Wadsworth.

Crampton, C. (2001). The mutual knowledge problem and its consequences for dispersed collaboration. *Organization Science.* 12: 346–371.

Cutler, S.W., & Daigle, D.A. (2002). Using business methods in the law: The value of teamwork among lawyers, *T. Jefferson L. Rev.* 25: 195–221.

DeStephen, R. & Hirokawa, R. (1988). Small group consensus: Stability of group support of the decision, task process, and group relationships. *Small Group Behavior.* 19:227–239.

Devine, D.J. (2012). *Jury decision making: The state of the science.* New York: New York University Press.

De Vries, K. & Manfred, F.R. (2005). Leadership coaching in action: The zen of creating high performance teams. *Academy of Management Executive.* 19(1): 61–76.

Dewey, J. (1910). How we think. Lexington, MA: D.C. Heath.

Doran, G.T. (1981). There's a S.M.A.R.T. way to write management's goals and objectives. *Management Review.* 70(11): 35–36.

Fink, C.F. (1968). Some conceptual difficulties in the theory of social conflict. *Journal of Conflict Resolution.* 12: 412–460.

Fink, L.D. (2004). Beyond small groups: harnessing the extraordinary power of learning teams. In L.K. Michaelsen, A. Bauman Knight & L.D. Fink (Eds.), *Team-based learning: A transformative use of small groups in college teaching* (pp. 3–26). Sterling VA: Stylus Publishing, LLC.

Firestein, R. (1990). Effects of creative problem solving training on communication behaviors in small groups. Small Group Research. 21: 507–521.

Fisher, R. & Sharp, A. (1999). *Getting it done: How to lead when you're not in charge.* New York: Harper Perennial.

Folger, J.P., Poole, M.S, & Stutman, R. K. (2009). *Working through conflict: Strategies for relationships, groups, and organizations* (6th ed.). Boston, MA: Pearson, Allyn & Bacon.

Forrester, R. & Drexler, A.B. (1999). A model for team-based organization performance. *Academy of Management Executive.* 13(3): 36–49.

Goleman, D. (2006). Social intelligence: The new science of human relationships. New York: Bantam Dell.

Goleman, D. et al. (2002). *Primal leadership: Realizing the power of emotional intelligence.* Boston: Harvard Business School Publishing,

Greenleaf, R.K. (2013). *Center for Servant Leadership.* Retrieved on March 8, 2013 from http://www.greenleaf.org/.

Hall, R.H. (1969). *Conflict management survey: A survey on one's characteristic reaction to and handling of conflicts between himself and others.* Monroe, TX: Teleometrics International.

Hastings, C., Bixby, P. & Chaudry-Lawton, R. (1987). The superteam solution: Successful teamworking in organisations (2d ed). Wiley, John & Sons, Inc.

Heineman, B.W. Jr. (2006). Law and leadership. *J. Legal Educ.* 56: 596–614.

Hickman v. Taylor. 329 U.S. 495 (1947).

Hirokawa, R.Y. & Scheerhorn, D.R. (1986). Communication in faulty group decision-making. In R.Y. Hirokawa & M.S. Poole, *Communication and Group Decision-Making.* Beverly Hills, CA: Sage.

Hofstede, G., Hofstede G.J., & Minkov, M. (2010). Cultures and organizations: Software of the mind (3rd ed.). New York: McGraw Hill.

Hollingsworth v. Perry. Petition for certiorari, U.S. Supreme Court No. 12–144 (2012).

Ivy, D.K. & Backlund, P. (1994). *Exploring genderspeak: Personal effectiveness in gender communication.* New York: McGraw-Hill.

Janis, I. (1989). *Crucial decisions: leadership in policymaking and crisis management.* New York: The Free Press.

Janis, I. (1983). *Groupthink: Psychological studies of policy decisions and fiascoes.* Boston: Houghton Mifflin.

Jarvenpaa, S. & Leidner, D. (1999). Communication and trust in global virtual teams. *Organization Science.* 10:791–815.

Johnson, D.W. & Johnson, F.P. (2006). *Joining together: Group theory and group skills* (9th ed.). Boston, MA: Allyn and Bacon.

Johnson, D.W. & Johnson, R.T. (2004). *Assessing students in groups: Promoting group responsibility and individual accountability.* Thousand Oaks, CA: Corwin Press.

Jones, E.E. & Nisbett, R.E. (1971). The actor and the observer: Divergent perceptions of the causes of behavior. In E.E. Jones, E. Kanouse, H.H. Kelley, R.E. Nisbett, S. Valins & B. Winer (Eds.), *Attribution: Perceiving the causes of behavior.* Morristown, NJ: General Learning Press.

Kaiser, P., Tullar, W. & McKowen, D. (2000). Student team projects by internet. *Business Communication Quarterly.* 63(4):75–82.

Katzenbach, J.R. & Smith, D.K. (2001). *The discipline of teams: A mindbook-workbook for delivering small group performance.* New York: John Wiley & Sons.

Katzenbach, J.R. & Smith, D.K. (1999). *The wisdom of teams: Creating the high performance organization* (2d ed.). New York: HarperCollins.

Kayworth, T. & Leidner, D. (2000). The global virtual manager: A prescription for success. *European Management Journal.* 18(2):183–194.

Kennedy, D. & Mighell, T. (2008). *The lawyer's guide to collaboration tools and technologies.* Chicago, IL: ABA Books.

Kennedy, J.W. Jr. (1998). Personality type and judicial decisionmaking. *Judges' Journal.* 37(4).

Kozan, M.K. (1997). Culture and conflict management: A theoretical framework. *The International Journal of Conflict Management.* 8: 338–360.

Kronman, A. (1993). *The lost lawyer: Failing ideals of the legal profession.* Harvard University Press: Cambridge, MA.

Kruempel, K. (2000). Making the right (interactive) moves for knowledge-producing tasks in computer-mediated groups. *IEEE Transactions on Professional Communication.* 43(2):185–195.

Law School Survey of Student Engagement, 2012 Annual Survey Results.

Lencioni, P. (2002). *The five dysfunctions of a team: A leadership fable.* San Francisco: Jossey-Bass, Inc.

Lewin, K. (1951). *Field theory in social science.* New York: Harper & Bros.

Lin, C., Standing, C. & Liu, Y.C. (2008). A model to develop effective virtual teams. *Decision Support Systems.* 45:1031–1045.

Lucas, R.E. & Donnellan, M.B. (2009). If the person-situation debate is really over, why does it still generate so much negative affect? *Journal of Research in Personality.* 43(3): 146–149.

Lumsden, G., Lumsden, D. & Wiethoff, C. (2010). *Communicating in groups and teams: Sharing leadership* (4th ed.). Boston, MA: Wadsworth.

Majchrzak, A., Rice, R., King, N., Malhotra, A. & Ba, S. (2000). Computer-mediated inter-organizational knowledge-sharing: Insights from a virtual team innovating using a collaborative tool. *Information Resources Management Journal.* 13:44–53.

Maznevski, M. L. & Chudoba, K. M. (2000). Bridging space over time: Global virtual team dynamics and effectiveness. *Organizational Science.* 11:473–492.

Meyerson, D., Weick, K.E. & Kramer, R.M. (1996). Swift trust and temporary groups. In R. M. Kramer & T. R. Tyler (Eds.). *Trust in organizations: Fron-*

tiers of theory and research (pp. 166–195). Thousand Oaks, CA: Sage Publications.

Moens, G.A. (2007). The mysteries of problem-based learning: combining enthusiasm and excellence. *University of Toledo Law Rev.* 38: 623–632.

Morrison, R.W. & Ashing, R. (2003). New effort on talent management. *Corp. Counsel.* 18(3).

Myers, I.B. (1998). *Introduction to type* (6th ed., rev. Kirby, L.K. & Myers, K.D.). Gainsville, FL: Consulting Psychologists Press, Inc.

Narko, K., Inglehart, E. & Zimmerman, C. (2003). From cooperative learning to collaborative writing in the legal writing classroom, Legal Writing 9:185. Reprinted in *The New Teacher's Deskbook. Legal Writing Institute Monograph Series.*

Nichols, M.P. (2009). *The lost art of listening: How learning to listen can improve relationships.* New York: Guilford Press.

Nicotera, A.M. & Dorsey, L.K. (2006). Individual and interactive processes in organizational conflict. In *The Sage handbook of conflict communication* (pp. 293–326). Thousand Oaks, CA: Sage Publishing.

Nischwitz, J. L. 2007. *Think again: Innovative approaches to the business of law.* Chicago, IL: ABA, Law Practice Management Section.

Northwestern University School of Law, Plan 2008. Retrieved March 9, 2013 from https://www.law.northwestern.edu/difference/NorthwesternLaw-Plan2008.pdf.

Nunamaker, J.F. Jr., Renig, B.A. & Briggs, R.O. (2009). Principles for effective virtual teamwork. *Communications of the ACM.* 52(4):113.

Osborn, A.F. (1963). *Applied imagination: Principles and procedures of creative problem solving* (3rd rev. edition). New York, NY: Charles Scribner's Sons.

Pachter, B. & Magee, S. (2000). *The power of positive confrontation: The skills you need to know to handle conflicts at work, at home and in life.* New York: Marlowe and Company.

Paul, A.M. (2004). *The cult of personality: How personality tests are leading us to miseducate our children, mismanage our companies, and misunderstand ourselves.* New York: Free Press.

Pauleen, D.J. (2003). An inductively derived model of leader-initiated relationship building with virtual team members. *Journal of Management Information Systems.* 20: 227–256.

Poole, M. S. (1983). Decision development in small groups, III: A multiple sequence model of group decision development. *Communication Monographs.* 50: 321–341.

Powell, A., Piccoli, G. & Ives, B. (2004). Virtual teams: A review of current literature and directions for future research. *The Data Base for Advances in Information Systems*. 35(1).

Putnam, L. & Folger, J.P. (1988). Communication, conflict and dispute resolution: /the study of interaction and the development of conflict theory. *Communication Research*. 15: 349–359.

Putnam, L. (1990). Reframing integrative and distributive bargaining: A process perspective. In R.J. Lewicki, B.H. Sheppard, and M.H. Bazerman (Eds.) *Research on negotiation in organizations* (Vol. 2). Greenwich, CT: JAI Press.

Redding, R.E. (2008) Book Review. J. Legal Educ. 58:312 [Reviewing M. M. Peters & D. Peters, (2007). *Juris types: Learning law through self-understanding. Gainsville FL: Center for Applications of Psychological Type, Inc.*].

Reilly, E.A. (2000). Deposing the 'Tyranny of Extroverts': Collaborative Learning in the Traditional Classroom Format. *Legal Education* 50: 593–614.

Rhode, D. & Packel A. (2011). *Leadership: Law, policy, and management. Amsterdam: Wolters Kluwer Law & Business.*

Richard, L. (2008). Herding cats: The lawyer personality revealed. *LAWPRO*, 7(1). Retrieved on March 8, 2013, from www.lawpro.ca/magazinearchives.

Richard, L.R. (2007). Question and answer. Retrieved on March 8, 2013 from http://www.hildebrandt.com/Documents.aspx?Doc_ID=2593.

Richard, L. (1993). The lawyer types: How your personality affects your practice. *ABA Journal*, 74–79.

Riskin, G. (2005). *The successful lawyer: Powerful strategies for transforming your practice.* Chicago, IL: ABA Books.

Rothwell, J.D. (2004). In mixed company: Communicating in small groups and teams. Belmont, CA: Wadsworth.

Rubinstein, H. (2008). *Leadership for lawyers* (2d ed.). Chicago, IL: ABA Books.

Ruble, T.L. & Thomas, K.W. (1976). Support for a two-dimensional model of conflict behavior. *Organizational behavior and human performance*. 16: 143–155.

Sarker, S. & Sahay, S. (2002). Information systems development by US-Norwegian virtual teams: Implications of time and space. *Proceedings of the thirty-fifth annual Hawaii International Conference on System Sciences* (pp. 1–10).

Sarker, S., Lau, F. & Sahay, S. (2001). Using an adapted grounded theory approach for inductive theory building about virtual team development. *Database for Advances in Information Systems*. 32: 38–56.

Saunders, C. S. (2000). Virtual teams: Piecing together the puzzle. In R. W. Zmud (ed.). *Framing the domain of IT management: Projecting the future through the past.* Pinnaflex.

Scallen, E. A. (2003). Evidence law as pragmatic legal rhetoric: Reconnecting legal scholarship, teaching and ethics. *Quinnipiac L. Rev.* 21: 813–890.

Schaub, J. (1995). Personality and perspective: Enhancing professional effectiveness. *Bench & Bar* 19: 23.

Scott, S. (2004). Fierce conversations: Achieving success at work & in life one conversation at a time. New York: The Berkeley Publishing Group.

Schutz, P. & Bloch, B. (2006). The "silo-virus": Diagnosing and curing departmental groupthink. *Team Performance Management.* 12: 31–43.

Shultz M. M. & Zedeck, S. (2011). Predicting lawyer effectiveness: Broadening the basis for law school admission decisions. *Law & Soc. Inquiry* 36: 620–657.

Sims, R. (1992). Linking groupthink to unethical behavior in organizations. *Journal of Business Ethics.* 11: 651–662.

Snowden, D. J. & Boone, M. E. (2009). A leader's framework for decision making. In *Harvard Business Review's Essential Guide to Leadership* (pp. 61–68).

Spears, L.C. (Ed.). (1995). *Reflections on leadership: How Robert K. Greenleaf's theory of servant leadership influenced today's management thinkers.* New York: John Wiley.

Spriggs II, J.F. & Stras, D.R. (2011). Explaining plurality decisions. *Georgetown Law Journal.* 99: 515–570.

Steil, L.K. (1997). Listening training: The key to success in today's organizations, in Michael Purdy & Deborah Borisoff, (Eds.) *Listening in everyday life: A personal and professional approach* (2d ed.). Lanham, MD: University Press of America.

Street, M. (1997). Groupthink: An examination of theoretical issues, implications, and future research suggestions. *Small Group Research.* 28: 72–93.

Stroebe, W. & Diehl, M. (1991). Productivity loss in idea-generating groups: Tracking down the blocking effect. *Journal of Personality and Social Psychology.* 61(3): 392–403.

Stroebe, W. Diehl, M. & Abakoumkin, G. (1992). The illusion of group effectivity. *Personality and Social Psychology Bulletin.* 18(5): 643–650.

Stuckey, R.T. et al. (2007). Best practices for legal education: A vision and a road map. Clinical Legal Education Association.

Suchan, J. & Hayzak, G. (2001). The Communication Characteristics of virtual teams: A case study. *IEEE Transactions on Professional Communication.* 44(3): 174–186.

Sullivan, W.M. et al. (2007). The Carnegie Found. for the Advancement of Teaching, Educating lawyers: Preparation for the profession of law.

Sweet, M. & Michaelsen, L.K. (2012). Critical thinking and engagement: Creating cognitive apprenticeships with team-based learning. In M. Sweet &

L.K. Michaelsen (Eds.), *Team-based learning in the social sciences and humanities: Group work that works to generate critical thinking and engagement* (pp. 5–32). Sterling, VA: Stylus Publishing, LLC.

Thomas, K.W. (1976). Conflict and conflict management. In M. Dunette (Ed.), *Handbook of industrial and organizational psychology* (pp. 889–935). Chicago, IL: Rand McNally.

Thomson, D.I.C. (2009). Law school 2.0: Legal education for a digital age. LexisNexis.

Toobin, J. (2007). *The nine: Inside the secret world of the Supreme Court.* New York: Doubleday.

Tuckman, B. & Jensen, M. (1977). Stages of small-group development. *Group and Organizational Studies.* 2: 419–427.

Tugend, A. (2009, August 28). For best results, take the sting out of criticism. *New York Times, Business Section.* Retrieved on March 8, 2013 from http://www.nytimes.com/2009/08/29/business/29shortcuts.html?emc=eta.

Twitchell, M. (1988). The ethical dilemmas of lawyers on teams. *Minn. L. Rev.* 72: 697–773.

Waldman, D.A. & Yammarino, F.J. (1999). CEO charismatic leadership: Levels-of-management and levels-of-analysis effects," *Academy of Management Review.* 24: 266–85.

Weisbord, E., Charnov, B.H. & Lindsey, J. (1995). *Managing people in today's law firm: The human resources approach to surviving change.* Westport, CT: Quorum Books.

White, R.K. & Lippett, R.O. (1960). *Autocracy and Democracy.* New York: Harper & Row.

Wolff, S.B., Pescosolido, A.T. & Druskat, V.U. (2002). Emotional intelligence as the basis of leadership emergence in self-managing teams. *Leadership Quarterly.* 13: 505–522.

Zimmerman, C. S. (1999). Thinking beyond by own interpretation: Reflections on collaborative and cooperative learning theory in the law school curriculum. *Ariz. St. J.* 31: 957–1020.

Zolin, R., Hinds, P. J., Fruchter, R. & Levitt, R. E. (2004). Interpersonal trust in cross-functional, geographically distributed work: A longitudinal study. *Information and Organization,* 13:1–26.

Zwier, P.J. (2006). *Supervisory and leadership skills in the modern law practice: Creating a learning organization.* Louisville, CO: National Institute for Trial Advocacy.

Index

153